The NEW GLUCOSE Revolution

Low GI Gluten-Free Eating Made Easy

The **NEW** **GLUCOSE** *Revolution*

Low GI Gluten-Free Eating Made Easy

The Essential Guide to the Glycemic Index and Gluten-Free Living

JENNIE BRAND-MILLER, PH.D.
KATE MARSH, R.D., C.D.E.
PHILIPPA SANDALL

Da Capo
∞
LIFE
LONG

A MEMBER OF PERSEUS BOOKS GROUP

Recipe testing and development by Diane Temple
Spice and herb blend recipes on pages 218–219 courtesy of Ian Hemphill, Herbie's Spices

This edition published by arrangement with Hachette Livre Australia.

The GI symbol a trademark of the University of Sydney that is recognized in Australia, the United States, and in other countries, is a public health initiative that provides consumers with a credible signpost to healthier food choices using the internationally recognized benefits of GI and sound nutrition. More information about the program is available at www.gisymbol.com.

Designed by Pauline Neuwirth, Neuwirth & Associates, Inc.
Set in 11.5 point Fairfield Light by the Perseus Books Group

Library of Congress Cataloging-in-Publication Data

Brand Miller, Janette, 1952-
The new glucose revolution low GI gluten-free eating made easy : the essential guide to the glycemic index and gluten-free living / Jennie Brand-Miller, Kate Marsh, Philippa Sandall.
p. cm. — (New glucose revolution series)
Includes index.
ISBN 978-1-60094-034-7 (pbk. : alk. paper) 1. Gluten-free diet—Recipes.
2. Celiac disease—Diet therapy—Recipes. 3. Glycemic index.
I. Marsh, Kate. II. Sandall, Philippa. III. Title.
RM237.86.B73 2008
641.5'638—dc22   2007048471

First Da Capo Press edition 2008
Published by Da Capo Press
A Member of the Perseus Books Group
www.dacapopress.com

Da Capo Press books are available at special discounts for bulk purchases in the United States by corporations, institutions, and other organizations. For more information, please contact the Special Markets Department at the Perseus Books Group, 2300 Chestnut Street, Suite 200, Philadelphia, PA 19103, or call (800) 255-1514, or e-mail special.markets@perseusbooks.com.

10 9 8 7 6 5 4 3 2

Contents

Foreword

*W*hen I was first told of the great news that *The New Glucose Revolution Low GI Gluten-free Eating Made Easy* was going to be written, I was thrilled. As a dietitian working in the area of celiac disease for a very long time, I have seen firsthand the struggle many have faced in making their gluten-free diet varied, nutritious, and enjoyable. As more and more people are aware of the importance of GI (the glycemic index), combining it with the gluten-free diet has created some confusion about what to buy, what to cook, and how to cook it! *Low GI Gluten-free Eating Made Easy* really does take away such uncertainties and difficulties—it is packed full of ideas on how to accomplish a great-tasting gluten-free low-GI diet.

There is no better team to write this enjoyable, informative, and delicious book. Kate Marsh, a well-respected dietitian, has both celiac disease and diabetes herself. She has joined forces with Jennie Brand-Miller—noted worldwide for her ground-breaking research involving the glycemic index—and Philippa Sandall, who has a unique vision for great publications.

Low GI Gluten-free Eating Made Easy is a book for many. It is ideal for people requiring both a gluten-free diet and a diet to assist with diabetes, heart disease, weight goals, or insulin control, and it appetizingly invites all people to incorporate low-GI cooking into their lifestyle.

But it is more than just a recipe book. I commend the authors for a marvelous job in compiling useful information for readers, including background to the gluten-free diet, glycemic index, and principles of healthy eating. The menu plans are so helpful. The comprehensive low-GI gluten-free food list at the back of the book is an invaluable resource. The information and recipes have been compiled with such careful attention to detail—this is a great reference book of all things low-GI and gluten-free.

I began taste testing the recipes myself with the Grilled Lemon Chicken Skewers, and very soon afterward I cooked the Squash, Ricotta, and Lentil Lasagna, and of course dessert! I could not turn the page past the Chocolate Almond Cake. My taste buds were happy and content—but it was hard to resist going back for more. I am sure you, as readers of the delicious recipes contained within, will wholeheartedly agree.

I hope you enjoy this as much as I have.

SUE SHEPHERD

Sue Shepard is an award-winning advanced accredited practicing dietitian who specializes in the treatment of dietary intolerances and is the author of several gluten-free cookbooks.

www.coeliac.com.au

Preface

*H*aving lived with type 1 diabetes since I was ten, and celiac disease for the past few years, I've experienced firsthand the difficulties of following a restricted diet. And as a dietitian working with many people with the same conditions, I am only too well aware of the challenges faced by anyone trying to eat gluten-free, let alone trying to manage their blood glucose levels.

In fact, in my work, I have found that many adults and children with celiac disease, in their attempt to follow a strict gluten-free diet, don't end up eating a particularly well-balanced diet.

And although for most people, the improvement in how they feel makes it easy to stick with their diet, I have also seen the struggle some have with:

- The lack of variety in their diet
- Feeling hungry all the time
- Running out of energy during the day.

That is why I have teamed up with Jennie and Philippa to write this book. Gluten-free or not, eating well is the key to our health and well-being, so it pays to get it right.

Low GI Gluten-free Eating Made Easy is for anyone with celiac disease or a gluten intolerance who wants to maximize their health and energy levels by eating well. If you want to ensure that you still get all the nutrients your body needs, feel satisfied after meals, enjoy a varied diet despite restrictions, and optimize your long-term health and well-being, then this book is for you.

WHY THIS BOOK IS IMPORTANT

Celiac disease is completely treatable through diet. But there is much more to your gluten-free lifestyle than focusing on foods you need to avoid. Eating well is the key to good health for everyone, and eating the right foods gives your body the fuel it needs to perform at its best and the energy to get through the day. It's also an important part of managing and preventing other long-term health problems, including diabetes, heart disease, and cancer, and a range of digestive problems.

Although it is great to see an ever-increasing range of gluten-free foods becoming available and making life easier for those with celiac disease, unfortunately many of them are highly processed and some are high in fat and added sugar—two ingredients that are naturally gluten-free!

Gluten-free diets also tend to have a high glycemic index (GI)—we explain what this is and why it matters in detail in Chapter 3. Many low-GI staples, such as whole-wheat kernel breads, pasta, barley, and oats, are eliminated because they contain gluten. The gluten-free alternatives, due to their ingredients and processing methods, are often quickly digested and absorbed, raising blood glucose and insulin levels and leaving you feeling hungry and often low on energy a few hours after eating.

What this means in practice is that many people following a gluten-free diet are rarely satisfied after meals and may feel hungry between meals, which can lead to overeating and weight gain. As far as we know, this is the first book that shows you how to incorporate low-GI carbs into your meals and reap their health benefits, including a reduced risk of prediabetes, type 2 diabetes, cardiovascular disease, and some types of cancer. A low-GI diet can also help people with diabetes manage their blood glucose levels. Since celiac disease is more common in people with type 1 diabetes, this is particularly important. Low-GI eating is for everybody, every day, every meal.

It can be difficult to get the right balance on a gluten-free diet, but it is certainly not impossible. In fact, we will show you just how easy it is in this comprehensive guide to what you should be eating, the things you need to leave out, and a fantastic selection of delicious recipes to tempt your taste buds.

KATE MARSH
Sydney, 2008

Once again, the team behind the New Glucose Revolution phenomenon has pulled together to bring you cutting-edge science and practical know-how to make a healthier, happier you. We are delighted to have Kate on board again (she helped us write *The New Glucose Revolution Guide to Living with PCOS* and *The New Glucose Revolution Low GI Vegetarian Cookbook*), bringing both her personal and professional experience of living and breathing a gluten-free diet. If you'd like to keep up to date with the latest GI science and GI values, subscribe to our free newsletter, GI News, at http:ginews.blogspot.com.

JENNIE BRAND-MILLER
and PHILIPPA SANDALL
Sydney, 2008

PART 1

Going Gluten-free

For many adults and children, gluten-free eating is a lifesaver. But if it's not well planned, the result can be an unbalanced, unhealthy diet low in whole grains and fiber and high in the fat and added sugar found in many of the gluten-free foods on supermarket shelves. And it is probably a high-GI diet too, because slowly digested staples such as grainy breads, pasta, muesli, and traditional rolled oats are off the menu.

·1·

Who Really Needs a Gluten-free Diet and Why

*S*ome people can't tolerate gluten. If you have celiac disease or dermatitis herpetiformis (a gluten-sensitive chronic skin condition) you need to eat a gluten-free diet. For life. If you have a gluten intolerance (non-celiac gluten sensitivity) you will need to reduce the amount of gluten in your diet.

Gluten is the protein found in the grains wheat, rye, barley, and triticale. Oats are frequently grown, harvested, milled, and processed alongside gluten-containing grains, so they may be contaminated with gluten. They also contain a glutenlike protein that some people with celiac disease react to. So, although research is ongoing, oats are currently not recommended for people with celiac disease.

UNDERSTANDING CELIAC DISEASE

We don't know how or why celiac disease occurs, but it seems clear that both the environment and genes play a part. For example, we do know that around 10 percent of all parents, brothers, sisters, or children (first-degree relatives) of someone with celiac disease will also have it. And if one identical twin has celiac disease, there is about a 70 percent chance the other twin will be affected.

We also know that it mainly affects Caucasians (people of European origin), but it occurs in India and some Middle Eastern countries, too. It is rarely diagnosed in Asian, African, and Native American populations.

We also now know it's not just an early childhood problem. Celiac disease affects children and adults of any age. Many people develop symptoms only as adults, and others have no obvious symptoms at all, making diagnosis very difficult. It is the most common and one of the most underdiagnosed hereditary autoimmune diseases.

In the United States and Canada, celiac disease affects up to one in every hundred people. On top of this, for every person diagnosed with celiac disease, there's likely to be six undiagnosed people with symptoms or complications attributable to it.

If you have celiac disease and you eat something that contains gluten, you will get an immune reaction in your small intestine. This damages your intestinal wall, reducing its ability to absorb nutrients from food and leading to deficiencies of the essential vitamins and minerals your body needs for growth, health, healing, and energy. In children, if it's not diagnosed and treated, celiac disease can affect growth and development. In adults, it can lead to long-term health problems including osteoporosis (due to calcium malabsorption), infertility, miscarriage, tooth decay, and an increased risk of cancers of the digestive system.

Celiac disease never goes away.

The good news is that you don't need drugs to deal with it; you can manage it effectively by following a strict gluten-free diet. By doing this, your intestinal wall will heal so nutrients can be absorbed, your symptoms will be resolved, and long-term health problems may be prevented.

Diagnosing It

Symptoms vary widely and some are very mild and nonspecific. Some people have all or many of the symptoms while others may have only a few or none at all. Typical symptoms include:

- Fatigue, weakness, and lethargy
- Low iron levels or unexplained anemia that does not improve or recurs after taking iron supplements
- Gas, bloating, and abdominal distension
- Stomach cramps
- Diarrhea
- Constipation
- Nausea and vomiting
- Weight loss
- Poor weight gain, delayed growth, and delayed puberty in children

Some less common symptoms in adults include:

- Easy bruising of the skin
- Mouth ulcers
- Infertility and miscarriages
- Muscle spasms/cramps due to low calcium levels
- Deficiencies of vitamins B_{12}, A, D, E, and K
- Dental problems
- Poor memory and concentration
- Bone and joint pains

If you have one or more of these signs or symptoms, make an appointment with your doctor for a checkup. He or she should refer you to a gastroenterologist who specializes in celiac disease.

Although blood tests that measure antibodies to gluten can be used to screen for celiac disease, you actually need to have a small bowel biopsy to diagnose it. This test looks at whether the lining of the small intestine shows the typical damage known as villous atrophy (inflammation of the villi, which line the surface of the small intestine) seen in those with celiac disease. A word of warning: It is important you don't jump the gun and start on a gluten-free diet before you have this test. If you do, the lining of your intestinal wall will repair and may not show any damage when the biopsy is taken, thus preventing a proper diagnosis.

UNDERSTANDING DERMATITIS HERPETIFORMIS

Dermatitis herpetiformis (DH) is also a genetic autoimmune disease caused by sensitivity to gluten. It causes an intensely itchy skin rash that looks like watery blisters or pimples. It generally presents in adult life and is more common in men than women and in people originally from some parts of northern Europe.

DH tends to appear over the kneecap, on the outer surface of the elbows, on the buttock area, around the ears, on the shoulder blades, and in the hairline and eyebrows. It usually occurs symmetrically (on both sides of the body).

As with celiac disease, you never get over it, but you can manage it with a gluten-free diet.

Diagnosing It

If you have DH, eating a food containing gluten triggers an immune response that deposits a chemical called immunoglobulin A (IgA) under the top layer of skin. Your dermatologist will need to take a skin biopsy to determine the presence of IgA deposits. Villous atrophy also occurs in people with DH.

It can take a year or two on a gluten-free diet for the IgA deposits under the skin to clear completely. But don't despair; medication can provide immediate relief from the itching and burning rash.

UNDERSTANDING GLUTEN INTOLERANCE

Gluten intolerance is a broad term, covering all kinds of sensitivity to gluten. In addition to those with celiac disease and DH, many people have a sensitivity to gluten but do not test positive for celiac disease. These people have what is called non-celiac gluten sensitivity, a condition in which the body does not tolerate large amounts of gluten.

If you have gluten intolerance you will generally need to reduce the amount of gluten in your diet, but you probably won't have to follow a strict gluten-free diet.

Diagnosing It

Symptoms may be similar to celiac disease and commonly include digestive symptoms such as diarrhea or constipation, gas, and bloating.

The most accurate way to diagnose gluten intolerance is by doing an elimination diet—this involves removing foods containing gluten for a specified time to see if symptoms resolve, then reintroducing foods containing gluten to see if the symptoms recur. This should be done under the guidance of a registered dietitian (RD) who specializes in food allergies and intolerance. However, it is important to establish whether you have celiac disease before you remove gluten from your diet.

UNDERSTANDING WHEAT INTOLERANCE

In addition to gluten intolerance, some people have an intolerance to wheat but are able to tolerate other gluten-containing grains such as barley, rye, and oats. Symptoms are similar to gluten intolerance and often include gas, bloating, and constipation or diarrhea.

Diagnosing It

The most accurate way to diagnose wheat intolerance is by doing an elimination diet—this involves removing foods containing wheat for a specified period of time to see if the symptoms go away, then reintroducing foods containing wheat to see if the symptoms recur. This should also be done under the guidance of a registered dietitian who specializes in food allergies and intolerances and, again, you should rule out celiac disease before starting an elimination diet.

Wheat Allergy

IT IS ALSO possible to have an allergy to wheat, although this is not common (it is more likely to be an intolerance) and is rarely as severe as other allergies, such as those to nuts, eggs, and seafood. A wheat allergy can be diagnosed using skin-prick testing—you should see your doctor if you suspect you have an allergy to wheat.

• 2 •

Gluten-free Ground Rules

*O*ur ground rules cover what's in, what's out, what tends to be missing from a gluten-free diet, and what you need to do about it.

Although it may seem like mission impossible to suddenly change the way you shop, cook, feed the family, and eat out, it's not the end of the world. There are plenty of great gluten-free foods to choose from. However, it may take more work and planning to start with.

In this chapter, we give you an idea of the sorts of foods you can enjoy to your heart's content, plus the ones you should leave off the menu. However, if you need to follow a strict gluten-free diet, we suggest as step one that you join your local celiac support group and take advantage of the up-to-date and comprehensive information it provides for members on shopping, cooking, and eating gluten-free. As for step two, it won't go amiss to brush up on your food-label reading skills (see page 12).

Our Favorite Gluten-free Food Web Sites:
- www.csaceliacs.org
- www.celiac.org
- www.celiac.ca
- www.gluten.net
- www.goglutenfree.com

WHAT'S IN?

There are many more foods you can eat than those you can't. For starters, some foods are naturally gluten-free, such as fruit and vegetables, legumes and nuts, many grains, meat, chicken, and fish (providing they haven't been processed or breaded). An increasing number of packaged gluten-free foods, such as breads, pastas, cookies, and crackers in supermarkets and health food stores, also make following a gluten-free diet much easier. Some major supermarkets have a gluten-free section where you can shop with confidence, although if you have diabetes you will still need to check nutritional labels for things like fats and total carbs.

The following foods are suitable for those on a gluten-free diet:

- Rice, corn, buckwheat, millet, sorghum, quinoa, amaranth, polenta, tapioca, sago
- Gluten-free breads and breakfast cereals
- Gluten-free pasta, rice noodles and vermicelli, buckwheat noodles, bean thread noodles
- Pure corn taco shells and tortillas
- Legumes (dried peas, beans, and lentils)—check canned varieties for gluten
- Plain nuts
- Fresh and frozen vegetables
- Fresh, frozen, canned, and dried fruit
- Fresh meat, chicken, fish, seafood, eggs, and plain tofu

▶ Gluten-free sausages and processed meats
▶ Plain milk, cheese, and yogurt (flavored varieties may contain gluten)
▶ Butter, margarine, and oils (except for wheat germ oil)
▶ Rice, corn, and buckwheat crackers and crispbreads
▶ Plain potato and corn chips; plain popcorn
▶ Gluten-free cakes and cookies
▶ Plain chocolate
▶ Jam, marmalade, honey, tahini (sesame seed paste), peanut butter, and other pure nut spreads
▶ Fresh and dried herbs and spices, salt, and pepper (check dried herb and spice mixes for gluten)
▶ All types of vinegar apart from malt vinegar
▶ Water, soda water, mineral water, soft drinks, fruit and vegetable juices, plain cocoa, milk, tea, coffee, wine, and spirits—but no beer (unless gluten-free), barley drinks, or malted milk drinks

WHAT'S OUT?

Wheat, rye, barley, oats, and triticale, and foods made from these grains, are out and need to be replaced with gluten-free alternatives. Gluten is also found in many foods you might not think about (such as sauces, dressings, stock, spreads, and processed meats), so it is important to become a label reader when shopping and to know exactly what to look for.

Here's a list (not definitive by any means) of foods that are out:

▶ Wheat (including semolina, couscous, spelt, and bulgur), rye, barley, and triticale, and any foods made from these including breads, cereals, pasta, noodles, crackers, cookies, cakes, muffins, and flour
▶ Oats and foods containing oats, such as muesli, muesli bars, granola, and granola bars

- Packaged stock (unless gluten-free)
- Many sauces, including soy sauce (unless gluten-free)
- Malt, barley malt, malt vinegar, breakfast cereals containing malt
- Textured vegetable protein (TVP) if derived from a gluten-containing grain
- Battered and crumbed foods, some commercial french fries, and potato wedges
- Beer, ale, stout (although gluten-free beer is now available)
- Maltodextrin from wheat (often found in soy milk, ice cream, and yogurts, especially flavored ones)
- Wheaten cornstarch
- Baking powder (unless gluten-free)
- Some candy
- Licorice (although gluten-free licorice is now available)
- Many flavored snacks including chips, corn chips, and rice crackers
- Coffee substitutes (e.g., Postum), malted milk drinks and flavors (e.g., Ovaltine); nondairy creamer
- Barley drinks

WHAT A GLUTEN-FREE DIET MAY MISS AND WHAT YOU CAN DO ABOUT IT

Adults and children on a strict gluten-free diet can miss out on the numerous health benefits of:

- Getting enough fiber
- Managing blood glucose levels with low-GI foods

Cracking the Gluten Code on Labels

Since the word *gluten* rarely appears on an ingredient list, you need to learn:

- Where less obvious sources of gluten may be found in foods
- Which ingredients are gluten-free
- Which are not

You will need to make a habit of reading food labels every time you shop to ensure that what ends up in your cart is safe for you to eat.

In Canada, the Food Inspection Agency requires that food labeled as "gluten-free" not contain any wheat, oats, barley, or rye, or their byproducts. However, in the United States the "gluten-free" label is not yet regulated at the time of this writing, although the U.S. Food and Drug Administration has proposed a voluntary label for gluten-free products.

On a Gluten-free Diet You Can Miss Out on Fiber

You need about 30 grams of fiber a day for good bowel health. Filling, high-fiber foods can also help you maintain a healthy weight by reducing hunger pangs. Plant foods are the only source of dietary fiber—it is found in the outer bran layers of grains, and in fruit, vegetables, nuts, and legumes. There are two types of fiber—soluble and insoluble.

Soluble fibers are the gel, gum, and often jellylike components of some foods, such as apples and legumes. By slowing down the time it takes for food to pass through the stomach and small intestine, soluble fiber can lower the glycemic response to a food. Good gluten-free sources include:

- Nuts and seeds
- Legumes (beans, peas, and lentils)
- Apples and pears
- Strawberries and blueberries
- Psyllium

Insoluble fibers are dry and branlike and commonly called roughage. All cereal grains and products that retain the outer coat of the grain they are made from are sources of insoluble fiber, but not all foods containing insoluble fiber are low GI. Insoluble fibers will lower the GI of a food only when they exist in their original, intact form. An example is whole grains, where the fiber acts as a physical barrier, delaying access of digestive enzymes and water to the starch within the cereal grain. Good gluten-free sources include:

- Whole-kernel grains (such as brown rice, quinoa, buckwheat, and millet)
- Nuts and seeds
- Most vegetables

On a Gluten-free Diet You Can Miss Out on the Benefits of Low-GI Foods

As stated in the introduction, gluten-free diets tend to have a high GI. This is because low-GI grain foods, such as whole-kernel breads, muesli, traditional rolled oats, pasta, and barley, are eliminated because they contain gluten, while the gluten-free alternative products are often quickly digested and absorbed, raising blood glucose and insulin levels.

Today we know that lowering the GI of your diet is one of the secrets to lifelong health. This is especially true for those people trying to prevent heart disease and type 2 diabetes. High-GI foods tend to cause spikes in your blood glucose levels, whereas foods with a low GI cause gentle rises. In Chapter 3 we look at carbohydrates, the GI, and the lifelong benefits of low-GI eating.

▪ 3 ▪

Gluten-free and Low GI— Why It Matters

*T*oday **we know** that it's important to be choosy about the type of carbohydrates we eat, because what we call their glycemic potency varies. This simply means that different carb foods will have dramatically different effects on blood glucose levels. The tool to help you choose the right type of carbs to trickle fuel into your engine and help you avoid the roller-coaster rise of "sugar highs" followed by "sugar lows" is the glycemic index, the GI.

The GI of a food reflects how fast its carbohydrates hit the bloodstream. It is based on scientific testing of real foods in real people, in the state in which they are normally consumed. It compares carbohydrates in different foods gram for gram. Foods with a low GI (55 and below) will have less of an effect on your blood glucose levels than eating foods with a high GI (70 and above).

▶ High-GI carbohydrates break down rapidly during digestion, releasing glucose quickly into the bloodstream.

▶ Low-GI carbohydrates break down slowly, releasing
glucose gradually into the bloodstream.

THE GI REVOLUTION

GI research has turned some widely held beliefs upside down.
Historically, carbohydrates were described by their chemical
structure: They were simple or complex. Sugars were simple
and starches were complex for no better reason than that sugars were small molecules and starches were big. By virtue of
their size, complex carbohydrates were assumed to be the slowly digested goodies, causing only a small rise in blood glucose
levels. Simple sugars, on the other hand, were assumed to be
the villains of the piece—digested and absorbed quickly, producing a rapid rise in blood glucose.

But these were just assumptions. And research has proved
them wrong. We now know that the concept of simple versus
complex carbohydrates is not a useful or true guide to how carbohydrates behave inside our bodies. And that's why the GI
caused a revolution.

Today we know the GI of hundreds of food items that have
been tested in healthy people (see the GI tables at the back of
the book for some examples). The findings rocked the boat in
many ways.

The first surprise was that the starch in foods such as white
or highly processed bread, potatoes, and many types of rice was
digested and absorbed very quickly—not slowly, as had always
been assumed.

Second, scientists found that the natural and refined sugars in foods such as fruit, dairy products, and ice cream did
not produce more rapid or prolonged rises in blood glucose,
as had always been thought. The truth was that most of the
sugars in foods, regardless of the source, actually produced
quite moderate blood glucose responses, lower than most of

the starches. Why? Because sugars are a mixture of molecules, and some of them have only a very slight effect on blood glucose levels.

So this is why you need to forget the old distinctions between starchy foods and sugary foods, or simple versus complex carbohydrates. These concepts are no help at all when it comes to managing your blood glucose levels. By learning about the GI you can base your food choices on sound scientific evidence that will help you choose the right type of carbohydrates for your long-term health and well-being.

How Can Starchy Foods Be Digested Quickly?

As we said earlier, foods containing carbohydrates that break down quickly during digestion have the highest GI values. Most modern starchy foods, especially processed ones such as many types of breads and breakfast cereals (gluten-free or not), are high-GI foods because the starch is fully gelatinized. This means it is highly soluble in digestive juices and easy for enzymes to attack. Because the digestion of starch produces its own weight as glucose, starchy foods can have a major impact on your blood glucose levels. Just like a flash flood when there's too much rain over a short period of time, rapid starch digestion results in blood glucose levels that rise quickly and create what you could call a "metabolic flood."

On the other hand, foods that contain carbohydrates that break down slowly, releasing glucose gradually into the bloodstream, have a low GI value. The starch in these foods is only partly gelatinized, and so it is more resistant to attack by digestive juices. The slow and steady digestion of low-GI foods produces a smoother blood glucose curve, greater feelings of fullness, and reduced metabolic disturbance. To show you the difference we have drawn a diagram—a picture can be worth a thousand words. The figure below shows the different effects of slow and fast carbohydrates on your blood glucose levels.

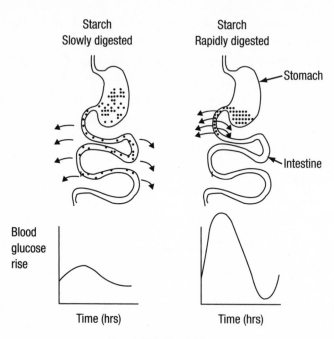

Figure 3.1—Starch Diagrams

The most important factor that determines the GI of a food is the final physical state of the starch (not the sugars). If the starch granules have swollen and burst (think puffed and flaked cereal products), they will be digested in a flash, even if the fiber content is high. On the other hand, if the starch is still present in "nature's packaging" (think whole intact grains and legumes), the process of digestion will take longer.

Over the past fifty to one hundred years, advances in food processing—such as high-speed milling, high-pressure extrusion cooking, and puffing technology—have had a profound effect on the carbohydrates we eat: They are much more rapidly digested and absorbed than the carbs our grandparents ate. It's one of the reasons why type 2 diabetes is far more common now than it was in the past.

But you don't have to eat only low-GI carbs to get the health benefit. We know that when a low- and a high-GI food are combined in one meal (such as lentils and rice), the overall blood glucose response is between the two. You can keep both your glucose and your insulin levels lower over the course of a whole day if you choose at least one low-GI food at each meal and for your snacks.

What This Means for You and Your Health

Lowering your insulin levels is one of the secrets to lifelong health. High insulin levels caused by eating foods with a high GI are undesirable. In the long term they promote high blood fat, high blood glucose, and high blood pressure and increase the risk of heart attack. Because of this, lowering the GI of your diet is significant in the long-term prevention of diabetes and heart disease and in improving your overall health. This is particularly relevant for anyone following a gluten-free diet—as we mentioned earlier in the book, gluten-free foods tend to have a higher GI. And if you have celiac disease, a gluten-free diet is for life.

Eating a low-GI diet has been scientifically proven to help people:

- With type 1 diabetes
- With type 2 diabetes
- With gestational diabetes (diabetes during pregnancy)
- Who are overweight
- Who are of normal weight but with excess abdominal fat
- Whose blood glucose levels are higher than desirable
- Who have been told they have prediabetes, "impaired glucose tolerance," or "a touch of diabetes"
- With high levels of triglycerides and low levels of HDL ("good") cholesterol
- With metabolic syndrome (the insulin resistance syndrome or syndrome X)

▶ Who suffer from polycystic ovarian syndrome (PCOS)
▶ Who suffer from fatty liver disease (NAFLD or NASH)

What Happens When You Eat Foods Containing Carbohydrates

WHEN YOU EAT foods containing carbohydrates, such as bread, breakfast cereals, rice, pasta, noodles, starchy vegetables (such as potatoes), and fruit, your body converts them into a sugar called glucose during digestion. The glucose is absorbed from your intestine into your bloodstream and becomes the fuel that circulates around your body.

As the level of blood glucose rises after you have eaten a meal, your pancreas gets the message to release a powerful hormone called insulin. Insulin drives glucose out of your blood and into the cells. Once inside, glucose will be channeled into various pathways simultaneously—it will be used as an immediate source of energy, converted to glycogen (a storage form of glucose), or converted into fat. Insulin also turns off the use of fat as the cell's energy source.

DIABETES AND THE GI

About 10 percent of people with celiac disease also have type 1 diabetes and need to manage their blood glucose levels. But managing blood glucose levels is something we all need to do in our "diabesity" world of expanding waistlines, because the higher the GI of your diet, the greater your risk of diabetes. Why? As we explained, foods with a high GI are digested quickly and cause a rapid rise in blood glucose and an outpouring of insulin. If you're constantly eating high-GI meals you end up with chronically high insulin levels, which eventually lead to insulin resistance, where the cells that normally respond to insulin become insensitive to it, so your body thinks it has to make even more insulin.

All too often, type 2 diabetes is diagnosed only once the pancreas (which produces insulin) is absolutely worn out and cannot maintain sufficient insulin production to normalize blood glucose. Before you get to that point, eating a moderately high-carbohydrate, low-GI diet can actually improve the function of your pancreas and glycemic control, and can therefore prevent the onset of type 2 diabetes.

For people with type 2 diabetes, following a low-GI diet can be as effective at lowering blood glucose as medication. A scientific analysis of fourteen studies from around the world of people with diabetes showed that low-GI diets improved glycemic control significantly more than high-GI or conventional diets. Improved glycemic control can prevent the onset and progression of diabetes complications.

On a daily basis, low-GI foods can minimize the blood glucose peaks and troughs that make life so difficult for people with diabetes. Since they are slowly digested and absorbed, low-GI foods reduce insulin demand—lessening the strain on the struggling pancreas of a person with type 2 diabetes and potentially lowering insulin requirements for those with type 1 diabetes. Lower insulin levels also have the benefit of reducing the risk of large blood vessel damage, thus reducing the risk of developing heart disease.

HEART HEALTH AND THE GI

These days, most of us are well aware of the importance of cutting back on saturated fat and choosing "good fats" for heart health. We now know that the higher the GI of your diet the greater your risk of heart disease. This is because a high level of glucose in the blood means:

- More glucose moves into cells lining the arteries, which causes inflammation, thickening, and stiffening of artery walls, so the blood vessels lose their elasticity
- Highly reactive, charged particles called "free radicals" (like "sparks") are formed and these destroy the machinery inside the cell, eventually causing the cell to wither and die
- Glucose sticks to cholesterol in the blood, which promotes the formation of fatty plaque and prevents the body from breaking down excess cholesterol
- Higher levels of insulin are present, which raises blood pressure and blood fats, while suppressing "good" (HDL) cholesterol levels

On the other hand, a diet rich in slowly digested, low-GI carbs, along with regular exercise, will reduce your risk of heart disease. By lowering your blood glucose after meals and reducing high insulin levels, you'll have:

- Healthier blood vessels that are more elastic, dilate more easily, and aid blood flow
- Thinner blood and improved blood flow
- More potential for weight loss and, therefore, less pressure on the heart
- Better blood fats—more of the good cholesterol and less of the bad

WEIGHT LOSS, THE GI, AND SATISFYING HUNGER

There is no doubt that reducing portion sizes and eating fewer calories will lead to weight loss. These days, we are eating less fat but getting fatter. Instead of eating fewer calories we are eating more, especially in the form of high-GI refined starches and sugars. The real solution to both weight loss and weight maintenance is to be choosy about the type of carbs you eat. Here are some reasons why:

▶ Eating high-GI carbs causes a surge of glucose in the blood. Although the body needs glucose it doesn't need this much all in one hit, so it secretes insulin to move the glucose out of the blood and store it in the cells. This drives blood glucose levels down and directs all incoming food to storage—glucose to glycogen and fat, and fats to fat storage.

▶ The action of insulin means blood glucose levels begin to decline rapidly.

▶ The brain detects falling blood glucose and, because it relies solely on glucose to keep us alive, it sends out hunger signals.

▶ The body would normally respond by releasing stored glucose for energy, but if insulin levels remain elevated (as they do in insulin resistance), the release of stored fuel is inhibited.

▶ Low levels of fuel and high levels of insulin can then trigger the release of stress hormones, such as adrenaline, which scour the blood for more glucose. This can translate to hunger, light-headedness, and shakiness. The only way to relieve the state of hunger is with another snack.

If you feel hungry all the time, here's how and why low-GI foods can help you turn off the switch:

▶ Low-GI foods are rich in carbohydrates—a far superior appetite suppressant than fat.

▶ Many low-GI foods are less processed, which means

they require more chewing, helping to signal satiety (fullness) to your brain.

▶ Low-GI foods are often accompanied by fiber, so they create a greater feeling of fullness in your stomach.

▶ They are more slowly digested, which means they stay in your intestines longer, keeping you feeling satisfied.

▶ They trickle glucose into your bloodstream slowly, helping you avoid the roller-coaster ride in blood glucose levels (a cycle of "sugar highs" followed by "sugar lows")

▶ Low-GI foods help overcome the body's natural tendency to slow down calorie burning (metabolic rate) while dieting.

MANAGING PCOS AND THE GI

Polycystic ovarian syndrome (PCOS) is thought to affect 5 percent to 10 percent of women in developed countries. Characteristics of the syndrome can include irregular periods, infertility, heavy body-hair growth, acne, excess weight gain, and difficulties losing weight. In many women it goes undiagnosed because the symptoms may be subtle, such as faint facial hair. Women with PCOS are also at higher risk of developing diabetes and cardiovascular disease.

Insulin resistance—where the body resists the normal actions of the hormone insulin—is at the root of PCOS for many women, and that's where the GI comes in. To overcome insulin resistance the body secretes more insulin than normal. Among other effects, high insulin levels cause an increased production of testosterone (male hormones) by the ovaries, causing a host of hormonal imbalances.

To manage PCOS symptoms effectively you need to make the change to low-GI eating and build more activity into your life. The benefits will include:

- Reducing PCOS symptoms
- Achieving and maintaining healthy weight
- Controlling blood glucose and insulin levels
- Boosting fertility
- Gaining control and quality of life

Why Insulin Resistance Is a Problem

ELEVATIONS IN BLOOD glucose after eating high-GI foods are followed by elevations in insulin. When insulin levels are frequently raised, the cells that usually respond to insulin become resistant to its signals. This means that glucose hangs around in the bloodstream at higher than normal concentrations, where it can damage cells.

A low-GI diet is invaluable in the management of insulin resistance because it will:

- Result in lower blood glucose after meals, and thereby
- Reduce the demand for insulin, which can
- Help appetite control and improve weight loss

·4·

Your Low-GI Food Finder

*L*ow-GI foods form the basis of a healthy diet. It is the way nature intended us to eat—low-fat, nutritious foods that satisfy hunger. Even on a wheat-free or gluten-free diet, you'll find that there are many low-GI gluten-free foods you can enjoy in four of the five food groups:

- Virtually all fruits and vegetables
- Whole-kernel grains in the breads and cereals group
- Legumes of all types in the meat and alternatives group
- Milk and yogurt among the dairy foods

WHICH FRUITS AND VEGETABLES TO CHOOSE

Temperate-climate fruits—apples, pears, citrus (oranges, grape-fruit), and stone fruits (peaches, plums, apricots)—all have low GI values.

Tropical fruits such as pineapple, papaya, cantaloupe, and watermelon tend to have higher GI values, but their glycemic load (we explain this on page 33) is low because they are low in carbohydrates. Bananas (so long as they are not overripe) have a low GI. So you can enjoy these tropical fruits in season, as they are excellent sources of antioxidants.

Think of vegetables as "free" foods—they are full of fiber, essential nutrients, and protective antioxidants that will fill you up without adding extra calories. Most are so low in carbohydrates they have no measurable effect on your blood glucose levels at all. In fact, leafy green and salad vegetables have so little carbohydrates that we can't test their GI. Even in generous serving sizes they will have no effect on your blood glucose levels.

Higher-carbohydrate starchy vegetables include sweet corn (which is actually a cereal grain), potatoes, sweet potatoes, taros, and yams, so watch the portion sizes with these. Most varieties of potatoes tested to date have a high GI, so if you are a big potato-eater, try to replace some with lower-GI starchy alternatives such as sweet corn, yams, or legumes.

Pumpkin, carrots, peas, parsnips, and beets contain some carbohydrates, but a normal serving size contains so little that it won't raise your blood glucose levels significantly.

WHICH BREADS AND CEREALS TO CHOOSE

The key is to look for less processed or refined products if you can—the ones with lots of whole-grain kernels and fiber. Remember, the whole point is to get your stomach to do the processing. Slowly.

A number of gluten-free breads, breakfast cereals, snack foods, and pastas are on the market. Because not many have been GI tested, here are some guidelines for selecting lower-GI options.

Bread

Most of the gluten-free breads, including rolls and wraps, tested have been found to have a high GI. But here is a tip: Check out the ingredients list and opt for breads that include chickpea- or legume-based flours and psyllium. For example, we know that chapatis made with besan (chickpea flour) have a low GI. If you make your own bread, try adding buckwheat kernels, rice bran, and psyllium husks to lower the GI.

Breakfast Cereals

Most gluten-free breakfast cereals, including rice, buckwheat, or millet puffs and flakes, have a moderate or high GI because they are refined, not whole-grain, foods. But you can reduce the GI if you serve them with fruit and yogurt and a teaspoon or two of psyllium to boost the fiber. Rice bran and buckwheat kernels have a low GI and can be used with other ingredients to make your own gluten-free muesli. See our recipe on page 81.

If you like cooked cereal, try quinoa porridge (made from whole quinoa grains) or make your own rice porridge (from a lower-GI rice). Add psyllium husks and rice bran, along with fruit and low-fat milk or yogurt. Again, see our recipes on pages 88–89.

Noodles and Pasta

There are several low-GI gluten-free options available in both fresh and dried varieties:

◗ Buckwheat (soba) noodles
◗ Cellophane noodles, also known as Lungkow bean thread noodles or green bean vermicelli, made from mung bean flour

▶ Rice noodles, made from ground or pounded rice flour

Most gluten-free pastas based on rice and corn (maize) tend to have moderate to high GI values. So opt for pastas made from legumes or soy—although they may be harder to find.

Pasta is best eaten al dente—it should be slightly firm and offer some resistance when you are chewing it. Al dente pasta has a lower GI, too, as overcooking boosts the GI. Although most manufacturers specify a cooking time on the package, don't take their word for it. Start testing about two to three minutes before the indicated cooking time is up.

You can further reduce the overall GI of your pasta meal by serving it (hot or cold) with sauces and salsas that contain some vegetables or legumes. See how we do it in our recipes in the Salads and Soups section (pages 142–166) and in the Main Dishes section (pages 170–193).

Whole Cereal Grains

Low-GI cereal grains for those on a gluten-free diet include buckwheat, quinoa, some varieties of rice (see below), and sweet corn. Currently there are no published values for amaranth, sorghum, and teff. Millet has a high GI.

Rice

Rice can have a very high GI value, or a moderate one, depending on the variety and its amylose content. Amylose is a kind of starch that resists gelatinization. Although rice is a whole-grain food, when it's cooked, the millions of microscopic cracks in the grains let water penetrate right to the middle of the grain, allowing the starch granules to swell and become fully "gelatinized," thus very easy to digest. Instant and quick cooking rices all tend to have a high GI.

So if you eat a lot of rice, opt for the lower-GI varieties with a higher amylose content, such as basmati rice (GI 58) and Uncle Ben's Converted Long-Grain White Rice (GI 45). You'll also find a number of lower-GI rice varieties listed on the database at www.glycemicindex.com or in the latest *New Glucose Revolution Shopper's Guide to GI Values*—there's an updated edition each year.

Brown rice is an extremely nutritious form of rice and contains several B-group vitamins, minerals, dietary fiber, and protein. The varieties tested to date tend to have a moderate or high GI, so try to combine this nourishing food with low-GI ingredients such as lentils or beans, or even in combination with wild rice. Wild rice (GI 57) is not rice at all, but a type of grass seed. Arborio rice, used mainly in risotto, releases its starch during cooking and has a medium GI.

What about Oats?

TO RECOMMEND THAT people with celiac disease avoid oats is controversial because some have been able to eat certain amounts of oats without any damage to their intestinal wall. Oats can add soluble fiber and nutrients to a gluten-free diet. Scientists are studying whether people with celiac disease can tolerate oats. Until the studies are complete, people with celiac disease should follow their physician's or dietitian's advice about eating oats.

Legumes (Pulses)

Dried or canned legumes, including beans, chickpeas, and lentils, are among nature's lowest-GI foods. They are high in fiber and packed with nutrients, providing protein, carbohydrates, B vitamins, folate, and minerals. Check canned varieties for gluten content.

When you add legumes to meals and snacks, you reduce the overall GI of your diet because your body digests them slowly. This is primarily because their starch breaks down relatively slowly (or incompletely) during cooking and they contain tannins and enzyme inhibitors that also slow digestion. So make the most of beans, chickpeas, lentils, and whole and split dried peas. You'll find we use them in many of our recipes—even cakes.

Nuts

Although nuts are high in fat (averaging around 50 percent of their content), it is largely unsaturated, so they make a healthy substitute for snacks such as cookies, cakes, pastries, potato chips, and chocolate. They also contain relatively few carbohydrates, so most do not have a GI value. Peanuts and cashews have very low GI values. Avoid varieties that are salted and cooked in oil—choose raw and unsalted. Also be aware that dry-roasted nuts may contain gluten.

Chestnuts are quite different from other nuts in that they are low in fat and higher in carbohydrates. Naturally gluten-free, they have recently been found to have a low GI, which makes them a great low-GI, high-fiber carbohydrate food for people with celiac disease. Roasted chestnuts are a nutritious snack or addition to meals and can also be ground into a flour for making breads, cakes, and pasta.

Low-fat Dairy Foods and Calcium-enriched Soy Products

Low-fat varieties of milk, yogurt, and ice cream, or calcium-enriched soy alternatives, provide you with sustained energy, boosting your calcium intake but not your saturated-fat intake. Check the labels of yogurts, ice creams, and soy milks, as some contain wheat-based maltodextrins, which should be avoided.

Cheese is a good source of calcium, but it is a protein food, not a carbohydrate, because its lactose is drawn off in the whey during production. This means that GI is not relevant to cheese. Although it is perfect for sandwich fillings, snacks, and toppings for gratin dishes, remember that cheese can also contribute a fair number of calories. Most cheese is around 30 percent fat, much of it saturated. Ricotta and cottage cheese are good low-fat choices.

What is Glycemic Load?

YOUR BLOOD GLUCOSE rises and falls when you eat a meal containing carbs. How high it rises and how long it remains high depends on the quality of the carbs (the GI) and the quantity. Glycemic load, or GL, combines both the quality and quantity of carbohydrate in one "number." The formula for calculating the GL of a particular meal is:

GL = (GI x the amount of carbohydrates) divided by 100

Although the GL concept has been useful in scientific research, it's the GI that has proven most helpful to people with diabetes. That's because a diet with a low GL, unfortunately, can be mixed—full of healthy low-GI carbs in some cases, but too low in carbs and full of the wrong sorts of fats, such as fatty meat and butter in others.

If you choose healthy low-GI foods—at least one in each meal and monitor the amount of carbohydrates—chances are you'll be on the right track to blood glucose control.

PART 2

How Do You Do It?

The best type of eating plan for most of us, including anyone on a gluten-free diet, is one that is low in saturated fat and contains sufficient protein and moderate amounts of carbohydrates, with most of the carbohydrate choices being low GI. It should have plenty of vegetables, salads, fruits, legumes, and whole grains. Here, we give you some tips on how to make the switch to low-GI, gluten-free eating, along with seven-day menus for adults, children, and vegetarians to help you and your family get started.

·5·

Going Gluten-free and Low GI

HEALTHY GLUTEN-FREE EATING GUIDELINES

Every day:

1. Eat seven or more servings of fruits and vegetables (at least five servings of vegetables and two of fruit).
2. Opt for gluten-free whole-kernel grain breads and cereals with a low GI.
3. Eat more legumes (dried beans, peas, and lentils).
4. Include nuts and seeds regularly in your diet.
5. Choose lean meats, omega-3-enriched eggs, and low-fat dairy products or calcium-enriched alternatives.
6. Eat more fish and seafood.
7. Opt for monounsaturated and omega-3 polyunsaturated fats, such as olive and canola oil and those found in fish, nuts, seeds, and avocados.

1.
EAT SEVEN OR MORE SERVINGS OF FRUITS AND VEGETABLES

Fruits and vegetables should form a major part of any healthy eating plan. They are rich sources of vitamins, minerals, antioxidants, and phytochemicals, all of which are important for good health and can help to protect you against cancer and cardiovascular disease. They are high in fiber and (apart from avocados and olives, which contain "healthy" monounsaturated fats) are very low in fat.

Variety is the key. Don't just stick with your favorites (apples, bananas, oranges) or the same old vegetable varieties, such as green beans, carrots, and peas. Why not buy something different each time you shop? Aim to make your plate or fruit bowl as colorful as possible. Ask your grocer what's in season right now.

Fruit—What's a Serving?

One serving is equivalent to:
- 1 medium piece of fresh fruit, such as an apple, banana, mango, orange, peach, or pear
- 2 small pieces of fresh fruit, such as apricots, kiwi fruit, or plums
- 1 cup of fresh diced or canned fruit pieces including grapes, berries, and strawberries
- 4–5 dried apricot halves, apple rings, figs, or prunes
- 1½ tablespoons raisins
- ¾ cup of 100 percent fruit juice, homemade or unsweetened

How Much a Day?

- **Smaller eaters:** 2 servings
- **Medium eaters:** 3 servings

▶ **Bigger eaters:** 4 servings

Vegetables—What's a Serving?

One serving is equivalent to:
▶ ½ cup cooked vegetables (other than starchy vegetables—potatoes, sweet corn, and sweet potatoes)
▶ 1 cup raw salad vegetables
▶ 1 cup vegetable soup (without cream!)
▶ 1 cup pure vegetable juice (such as tomato juice)

How Much a Day?

Even the smallest eater should aim to eat five or more servings of vegetables every day, including fresh and frozen vegetables, vegetable juices, and soups. This is a minimum of 2½ cups of cooked vegetables or 4 cups of salad.

Starchy Vegetables—What's a Serving?

Starchy vegetables such as sweet potatoes, potatoes, and sweet corn are higher in carbohydrates, so their GI and serving size are more relevant. One serving is equivalent to:
▶ 1 medium potato (slightly smaller than a tennis ball)
▶ ½ cup mashed potatoes
▶ ½ cup sweet potatoes
▶ ½ cup sweet corn kernels
▶ ½ ear sweet corn
▶ ½ cup taros or yams
▶ 1 large parsnip

How Much a Day?

The following is recommended in addition to the five or more vegetable servings:

- **Smaller eaters:** 1 serving
- **Medium eaters:** 3 servings
- **Bigger eaters:** 4 servings

Get Your Seven Servings a Day

Breakfast
- Include fruit (fresh, canned in natural juice, or dried) with your breakfast cereal.
- Try a fresh-fruit smoothie for a quick but satisfying breakfast meal.
- For a more substantial breakfast, add some vegetables on your low-GI, gluten-free toast—try asparagus, mushrooms, tomatoes, and onions, or sliced tomato and avocado.
- Mushrooms, asparagus, and tomatoes are also great added to omelets.

Lunch
- On your gluten-free sandwich, add plenty of salad vegetables, such as tomatoes, lettuce, cucumbers, sprouts, beets, grated carrots, and bell peppers.
- Try the same with toasted sandwiches. Go for tomatoes, peppers, mushrooms, sweet potatoes, olives, zucchini, and eggplant.
- Use mashed avocado as a spread on your sandwich instead of mayonnaise or butter.
- Salads are a great way to fill up at lunchtime and the combinations are endless. Don't stick with lettuce, tomato, and cucumber; try adding snow peas, peppers, sweet corn, green beans, steamed broccoli, asparagus, roasted sweet potatoes and eggplant, sundried tomatoes, and a few cubes of avocado or some olives.
- During colder weather, soups are a great way to get more vegetables into your diet. Try pumpkin, sweet potato, lentil, split pea, minestrone, or tomato.

Dinner

▶ Include vegetables or salads with all main meals. Serve them steamed, seasoned with fresh or dried herbs, or with a dressing made from olive oil, lemon juice, balsamic vinegar, and garlic.

▶ Always have some frozen vegetables handy for when you don't have time to shop for fresh varieties.

▶ If you don't like vegetables on their own, add them to stir-fries, curries, and casseroles or grated into ground meat.

▶ Choose vegetable-based dishes when eating out or ask for a side salad with your meal.

Snacks and Desserts

▶ Fruit and grated vegetables such as carrot and zucchini can be added into cakes and muffins.

▶ Choose fruit for snacks. It's widely available, inexpensive, easy to eat, and doesn't contain the added fat and sugar found in many other snack foods.

▶ Serve raw vegetables such as celery, carrot, cucumber, bell pepper, broccoli, or cauliflower florets as a snack served with a low-fat dip or salsa.

▶ Make fruit the basis of your desserts. Try baked apples, fruit crumbles, and canned fruit with low-fat pudding, yogurt, or ice cream.

2.
OPT FOR GLUTEN-FREE WHOLE-KERNEL GRAIN BREADS AND CEREALS WITH A LOW GI

Whole-kernel grain breads and cereals have many health benefits. Most have a lower GI than refined cereal grains and they are nutritionally superior, containing higher levels of fiber, vitamins, minerals, and phytochemicals. We know from studies that a higher consumption of cereal fiber and whole grains is associated with a reduced incidence of type 2 diabetes, cancer, and heart disease.

Eating these higher-fiber foods can help you lose weight, too, because they fill you up sooner and leave you feeling full for longer. They also improve insulin sensitivity and lower insulin levels. When this happens, your body makes more use of fat as a source of fuel. What could be better when you are trying to lose weight?

Replacing processed grains and cereals for those with a lower GI is a key part of making the change to a healthy, low-GI diet.

Watch That Glucose Load with Rice, Noodles, and Pasta

IT'S ALL TOO easy to overeat these foods, so keep portions moderate. Even if it has a low GI value, eating too much will have a marked effect on your blood glucose. So instead of piling your plate with rice, noodles, or pasta, fill it with vegetables and a little meat, chicken, fish, or tofu. For example, a cup of rice combined with plenty of mixed vegetables and a little protein food can turn into three cups of a rice-based meal and fit easily into any adult's daily diet.

Breads and Cereals—What's a Serving

One serving is equivalent to:
- 1 slice gluten-free bread (sandwich thickness) or ½ gluten-free bread roll
- ½ cup gluten-free breakfast cereal or muesli
- ½ cup cooked rice or other small gluten-free grain such as quinoa; or cooked gluten-free pasta or noodles

How Much a Day?

- **Smaller eaters:** 4 servings
- **Medium eaters:** 6 servings
- **Bigger eaters:** 8 servings

Enjoy More Gluten-free Breads and Cereals

Breakfast

- For sweetness, add some stewed apple, a few raisins, and a sprinkle of cinnamon to quinoa or brown-rice porridge. Top with low-fat milk or soy milk.
- In warmer weather, choose gluten-free cold cereals based on rice bran, psyllium, and buckwheat, or use these grains to make your own muesli (see recipe page 81).
- For those who prefer toast, choose gluten-free whole-grain varieties and those labeled low-GI or carrying the GI symbol.

Lunch

- For sandwiches, go for whole-grain gluten-free breads and wraps.
- Buckwheat or quinoa can be used to make gluten-free tabbouleh to add to wraps and sandwiches.
- Rice vermicelli noodles can be added to Thai salads, rice paper rolls, or Asian soups.

Dinner

- Choose Asian noodles such as rice, bean thread, or soba (buckwheat) noodles in place of rice, but always check that they are completely gluten-free.
- Try lower-GI rices, such as basmati and Uncle Ben's Converted Long-Grain White Rice.
- Buckwheat and quinoa can be added to soups and casseroles or used to make salads.

Snacks and Desserts

▶ Gluten-free raisin bread/toast with ricotta makes a satisfying snack for those with a sweet tooth.

▶ Make muffins using rice bran, buckwheat, and psyllium husks, fruit or dried fruit, and nuts or almond meal.

▶ For dessert, try a fruit crumble topped with rice bran cereal or a suitable crushed low-GI gluten-free cereal, or creamed rice made with a low- or lower-GI rice.

3.
EAT MORE LEGUMES

Legumes are high in fiber—both soluble and insoluble. They are also packed with nutrients, providing a valuable source of protein, carbohydrates, B vitamins, folate, and minerals. Sprouted dried beans such as mung, soy, chickpeas, and lentils, are excellent sources of vitamin C and are great eaten raw in a salad or stir-fried.

Legumes are an important part of the healthy, low-GI way of eating. They're particularly important for those on a gluten-free diet because they can provide much of the fiber and nutrients found in the gluten-containing grains that you can no longer eat.

What Are Legumes?

Legumes (also known as pulses) are the edible dried seeds—such as beans, peas, and lentils—found inside the mature pods of leguminous plants. Nutritionally, they are quite different from fresh, young green beans and peas, which don't have as much protein or fiber because of their high water content.

Thanks to their tendency to cause intestinal gas, there has been a bad odor about legumes, and lots of jokes. But not all legumes make you gassy and not everyone has the problem. Cooking legumes in fresh water (not in the water you soaked them in) and rinsing the canned varieties helps. Eat them regularly—it can improve your tolerance.

Canned legumes are ready to use and only need heating through. Meals based on these are much faster to prepare than meat-based meals, but check the label for wheat-based thickeners—these should be avoided.

Tofu (soybean curd) is an easy way of using soybeans. It has a mild flavor but absorbs the flavors of other foods, making it delicious when it has been marinated in tamari, ginger, and garlic and tossed into a stir-fry. Tofu contains very few carbohydrates, so it doesn't have a GI.

Legumes—What's a Serving?

- One serving is equivalent to ½ cup of cooked beans, lentils, chickpeas, or cooked whole dried or split peas.

How Much a Week?

- Incorporate legumes into your meals at least twice a week as a starchy vegetable—more often if you are a vegetarian.

Make These "Superfoods" a Regular Part of Your Low-GI Diet

Breakfast

- Baked beans on gluten-free toast make an easy and satisfying breakfast.
- Try scrambling silken tofu in place of eggs. Add some fresh or dried herbs and chopped tomato, and sauté in a little olive oil.

Lunch

- Lentil, split pea, or minestrone soup all make a satisfying winter lunch.
- Baked-bean toasted sandwiches on gluten-free bread are an easy all-time favorite.
- Add a can of three-bean mix or some chickpeas to a salad to really fill you up.
- Lentils or chickpeas can be mashed and made into burgers, served on a gluten-free roll or wrap.
- Spread hummus (made from chickpeas) on your gluten-free sandwich or wrap in place of butter.

Dinner

- Add red kidney beans to ground meat and serve with pure corn taco shells, tortillas, or gluten-free pasta or rice.
- Chickpeas have a nutty flavor and team well with curries and stir-fries.
- Make some dahl (lentils or split peas cooked with spices) to accompany your next curry.
- Green soybeans (edamame) are a tasty addition to a stir-fry. They are available frozen in most grocery stores.
- Add cannellini beans, cranberry beans, or black-eyed peas to stews and casseroles.
- Firm tofu can be cubed, marinated, and added to stir-fries or threaded onto skewers with vegetables to make kebabs for the grill.
- Substitute canned lentils for some of the ground meat in spaghetti Bolognese or a meat loaf.

Snacks and Desserts

- Silken tofu can be used in place of cream cheese to make desserts such as cheesecake.

- Roasted chickpeas or soybeans (dubbed chick nuts and soy nuts) make a tasty and satisfying snack.
- If you are really hungry, try a small can of baked beans or four-bean mix as a snack.
- For a healthy dip, go for hummus or bean purée with carrot and celery sticks.

Cooking with Legumes

Dried legumes: Dried beans and peas need soaking and cooking before you use them in your meals. Lentils and split peas cook much faster and don't need soaking.

- To soak beans, rinse and place them in a saucepan and cover with two to three times their volume of cold water. Set aside to soak overnight or throughout the day. If time is limited, take a shortcut by adding three times the volume of water to rinsed beans, bring to a boil for a few minutes, then remove from heat, and set aside to soak for an hour.
- To cook, drain off the soaking water, add fresh water, and bring to a boil, then simmer until beans are tender. Use the directions on the package as a time guide.
- Don't add salt to the cooking water. It slows down water absorption, increasing cooking time.
- Don't cook beans in the water they have soaked in. Substances that contribute to flatulence are leached from the beans into the soaking and cooking waters.

Canned legumes: Most legumes are available canned, making cooking with beans quick and easy. One 14-ounce can of beans substitutes for ¾ cup of dried beans. Check the label to avoid those with wheat-based thickeners.

4.
INCLUDE NUTS AND SEEDS REGULARLY IN YOUR DIET

Like legumes, nuts are a good food to include regularly. They are high in fiber and contain a range of important vitamins and minerals that can be harder to get on a gluten-free diet. They are a healthy choice because they contain:

- Very little saturated fat (the fats are predominantly mono- or polyunsaturated)
- Dietary fiber
- Vitamin E, an antioxidant believed to help prevent heart disease
- Folate, copper, and magnesium, nutrients thought to protect against heart disease

Walnuts and pecans also contain some omega-3 fats, while linseeds (flaxseeds) are rich in omega-3s, lignans, and plant estrogens. When freshly ground, linseeds have a subtle nutty flavor, making them a great addition to breads, muffins, cookies, and cereals.

Remember to choose the unsalted variety—salted nuts are usually roasted in saturated fat. And stick to a handful a day if you are watching your weight.

Nuts—What's a Serving?

One serving provides 10 grams of fat (apart from chestnuts, which are almost fat-free) and is equivalent to:

- ½ ounce (about 10 small or 5 large) nuts
- 1 tablespoon of seeds
- 1 tablespoon peanut butter or nut spread

How Much a Day?

Aim for a small handful (no fingers) of nuts most days.

- **Smaller eaters:** 1 serving most days
- **Medium eaters:** 1 serving a day
- **Bigger eaters:** 1–2 servings most days

Easy ways to eat more nuts and seeds

Breakfast
- Sprinkle a mixture of nuts and seeds over your cereal.
- Use a spread such as peanut, almond, or cashew butter on your toast in place of butter or margarine.

Lunch
- Add a handful of walnuts or pine nuts to your salad.
- Tahini (sesame seed paste) can be used as a spread on sandwiches or in salads in place of mayonnaise.

Dinner
- Add nuts and seeds to your favorite meals—try peanuts or sesame seeds in a stir-fry, cashews in a curry, crushed macadamias with fish or chicken, or roasted chestnuts with pasta.
- Pesto (ground pine nuts with basil, garlic, and olive oil) makes a good pasta sauce or accompaniment to meat or fish.
- Tahini can be used as an alternative to sour cream on potatoes or drizzled over roasted vegetables.

Snacks and Desserts
- Enjoy nuts as a snack. Just be careful not to eat too many. Limit them to one small handful (about ½ ounce) each day.

▶ Gluten-free crackers, rice cakes, or toast with nut spread make a satisfying snack.

▶ Nuts and seeds can be added to baked goods. Try walnuts, hazelnuts, almond meal, and ground chestnuts in cakes and muffins, and sunflower seeds, pumpkin seeds, sesame seeds, and linseeds (flaxseeds) in bread.

5.
CHOOSE LEAN MEATS, OMEGA-3 EGGS, AND LOW-FAT DAIRY

Reducing your intake of saturated fat doesn't mean that you need to avoid red meat and dairy products. They are good sources of protein, iron, and calcium.

If you enjoy meat, we suggest eating lean red meat two or three times a week and accompanying it with salad and vegetables. Trim all visible fat from meat and remove the skin (and the fat just below it) from chicken. Game meat such as rabbit and venison is not only lean but is also a good source of omega-3 fatty acids. So are organ meats such as liver and kidney. If you choose not to eat red meat or are trying to reduce your intake, legumes and tofu are good alternatives. They can provide the protein, iron, and zinc also found in red meat.

Replacing full-fat dairy foods with reduced-fat, low-fat, or fat-free varieties will also help you reduce your overall saturated-fat intake. Dairy products, including milk, yogurt, and cheese, are among the richest sources of calcium in our diet. They also provide protein and a number of important vitamins and minerals, such as vitamin B_{12}, phosphorus, magnesium, and zinc.

If you are lactose intolerant or prefer not to eat dairy products, you could choose calcium-fortified soy products such as soy milk and soy yogurt. Soy products contain mostly polyunsaturated fat, and the protein in soy products can help to lower cholesterol levels. They are also a source of omega-3 fatty acids and phytoestrogens. However, check the labels on these products, because some soy milks contain gluten, usually derived from wheat-based maltodextrin.

What about eggs and cholesterol? We used to think that eating high-cholesterol foods such as eggs, shrimp, and other shellfish would raise our blood cholesterol levels. We now know that our liver compensates for the increased cholesterol intake by reducing cholesterol production. This means that most people could eat an egg a day, for example, without harming their heart. However, a small percentage of people have an inherited condition called familial hypercholesterolemia, which impairs this self-regulation.

To enhance your intake of omega-3 fats, we suggest that you eat omega-3-enriched eggs if you can find them. These enriched eggs are produced by feeding hens a diet that is naturally rich in omega-3s (including canola and linseeds or flaxseeds).

Lean Meat, Chicken, and Eggs—What's a Serving?

One serving is equivalent to:

- 3½ ounces raw lean meat or chicken
- 2 medium eggs
- 1 small pork chop, visible fat trimmed
- ½ cup cooked lean ground beef
- ½ skinless chicken breast
- 1 large chicken drumstick

How Much a Day?

Although they're nutritious, meat, chicken, and eggs do not have to be a part of everyone's diet. After all, there are countless healthy vegetarians in the world. For meat eaters, we suggest eating lean meat three times a week, plus eggs or skinless chicken once or twice a week, accompanied by plenty of salad and vegetables.

- **Smaller eaters:** 1–2 servings a day
- **Medium eaters:** 2–3 servings a day
- **Bigger eaters:** 3 servings a day

Dairy Foods—What's a Serving?

One serving is equivalent to:

- 1 cup low-fat milk
- 1 cup calcium-enriched low-fat soy milk
- 6-ounce tub low-fat yogurt or calcium-enriched soy yogurt
- 1½ ounces or two slices reduced-fat hard cheese, such as cheddar
- 1 cup low-fat pudding is a calcium-equivalent option but is higher in calories, so don't rely on it routinely.

How Much a Day?

Everyone should aim to eat or drink at least three servings of dairy foods or calcium-enriched soy products per day to meet their calcium needs. Postmenopausal women need three to four servings each day due to increased calcium needs.

- **Smaller eaters:** 3 servings
- **Medium eaters:** 3 servings
- **Bigger eaters:** 3–4 servings

Including Lean Meats and Low-fat Dairy in Your Diet

Breakfast
- Try poached or scrambled eggs on toast or an omelet.

▶ Fruit smoothies make a great breakfast when you are on the go.

▶ Yogurt is a tasty accompaniment to muesli or fruit salad.

Lunch

▶ Gluten-free sandwiches and rolls can be filled with chicken and avocado; lean roast beef and mustard; turkey and cranberry sauce; sliced lamb with hummus; egg and lettuce; or lean ham and salad.

▶ If you prefer toasted sandwiches (a better choice when using most gluten-free breads), try chicken and avocado; ham, cheese, and tomato; or ricotta, sun-dried tomato, and arugula.

▶ Dress up your salad with lean roast meat, sliced chicken breast (no skin), a boiled egg, or some cubes of low-fat feta.

▶ Frittata made with eggs, low-fat milk, chopped vegetables, lean ham, fresh herbs, and low-fat cheese make a tasty weekend lunch or brunch served with salad.

▶ Soups are a great winter warmer—try chicken and sweet corn, beef and vegetable, or pea and ham.

▶ For a variation on your usual sandwich, try a gluten-free wrap filled with hummus, buckwheat tabbouleh and sliced chicken breast or roast lamb.

Dinner

▶ Go for lean meats—marinate and grill or pan-fry with a little olive or canola oil.

▶ Beef and chicken can be sliced into strips and stir-fried with vegetables.

▶ For the grill, choose lean steak, marinated chicken breast, or kebabs.

▶ Use lean meats in curries and casseroles. If you have time, cook the meal the day before, refrigerate, and then skim fat from the top the next day before reheating to serve.

‣ Low-fat plain yogurt and ricotta mixed with chives make a low-fat alternative to sour cream on vegetables or Mexican food.

Snacks and Desserts

‣ Fruit smoothies or low-fat milkshakes make a satisfying calcium-packed snack.

‣ Yogurt is always a quick and easy option.

‣ Try a glass of gluten-free hot chocolate to satisfy those chocolate cravings.

‣ Ricotta can be used as a topping on gluten-free crackers or a spread on fruit bread.

‣ For dessert, add a spoonful of gluten-free low-fat pudding, frozen yogurt, or ice cream to fruit.

‣ Low-fat ricotta can also be used in cheesecakes or as a topping for fresh fruit.

‣ Low-fat buttermilk can be used in baking and desserts.

Why Do I Never See a GI Value for Meat or Cheese?

THE FOODS WE eat contain three main macronutrients—protein, carbohydrates, and fat. Some foods, such as meat, are high in protein, while bread is high in carbohydrates and butter is high in fat. It is necessary for us to consume a variety of foods (in varying proportions) to provide all three nutrients, but the GI applies only to carbohydrate-containing foods. It is impossible for us to measure a GI value for foods that contain negligible carbohydrates. These foods include meat, fish, chicken, eggs, cheese, nuts, oil, cream, and butter. There are other nutritional aspects you should consider when choosing these foods, such as the amount and type of fats they contain.

6.
EAT MORE FISH AND SEAFOOD

Fish, particularly oily fish, is the best source of long-chain omega-3 fatty acids—fats that offer valuable health benefits. Long-chain omega-3s can help reduce blood clotting and inflammatory reactions, and studies have shown a link between regular fish consumption and a reduced risk of coronary heart disease. In fact, just one serving of fish a week may reduce the risk of a fatal heart attack by 40 percent. Our bodies make only small amounts of these fatty acids, so we rely on dietary sources, especially fish and seafood, for them. You should try to eat fish at least twice a week. Fresh fish that contains the highest amounts of omega-3 fats include:

- Swordfish
- Atlantic salmon
- Tuna
- Sardines
- Herring
- Atlantic, Pacific, and Spanish mackerel (blue mackerel)

Canned fish can also provide omega-3 fats, good sources being:

- Mackerel
- Salmon
- Sardines
- Tuna

Try to choose varieties canned in spring water where possible. If you choose fish canned in oil, opt for those in olive or canola oil.

Just remember not to eat fish cooked in solid (saturated) fat. That means avoiding fried fish from fast-food restaurants, even if they say it's cooked in vegetable oil.

Fish and Seafood—What's a Serving?

One serving is equivalent to:

▶ 5 ounces raw fish or seafood
▶ 4 ounces grilled or steamed fish
▶ 3½ ounces canned fish (drained)

How Much a Week?

Eat fish—including fresh, frozen, canned, and smoked—at least twice a week, as an alternative to a serving of meat, chicken, or eggs.

Tips to Help You Increase Your Intake of Fish

Breakfast

▶ Sardines on toast are filling and will give you a good dose of omega-3s.
▶ Try an omelet with smoked salmon or trout.

Lunch

▶ Add tuna or salmon to a gluten-free sandwich or salad.
▶ For something different, add salmon or tuna patties to a gluten-free roll with lettuce and avocado.
▶ Grilled fish with salad makes a healthy lunch choice when eating out.

Dinner

▶ Homemade fish and chips is a quick and easy meal to prepare. Wrap fish in foil with lemon juice and herbs and bake in the oven. Make sweet potato chips by slicing and brushing or spraying with olive oil, and baking on a tray in the oven. Serve with salad or steamed vegetables.

▶ Try adding tuna, salmon, or a seafood mix to gluten-free pasta with a tomato sauce and some vegetables.

▶ Grilled fish makes a healthy alternative to sausages and fatty meats.

▶ Use fresh salmon in a stir-fry, as it holds its shape.

7.
OPT FOR MONOUNSATURATED AND OMEGA-3 POLYUNSATURATED FATS AND OILS, SUCH AS OLIVE, PEANUT, AND CANOLA OILS

It is not necessary, or beneficial, to cut all fats out of your diet. In fact, some fat is essential for your health, as it provides essential fatty acids and carries fat-soluble vitamins and antioxidants. So it's fine to use small amounts of oil in cooking and salad dressings, but it is important to choose the right ones. If you don't use oil, you can still get these "good" fats by eating nuts, seeds, avocados, olives, and fish.

Although it is generally recommended that you replace saturated fats with either polyunsaturated or monounsaturated fats, there is something else to keep in mind. Omega-3 fats are one type of polyunsaturated fat (found mainly in oily fish but also in some plant foods including linseeds [flaxseeds], linseed oil, walnuts, canola oil, and soy products) that we know have many health benefits. But to make good use of the omega-3 fats in your diet it is important that you don't have too many omega-6 fats (the other type of polyunsaturated fat)—the ratio between them is important. Most people have too much omega-6 (found in most vegetable oils and margarines including sunflower, safflower, and grapeseed as well as most nuts and seeds) and too little omega-3.

To improve this balance we recommend having a regular source of omega-3 fats in your diet and cooking most of the time with monounsaturated oils rather than the polyunsaturated variety. These include:

Olive oil, which is high in monounsaturated fats and low in saturates with a minimal polyunsaturated fat content. This is an advantage, as it allows our bodies to make greater use of the omega-3 fats we obtain from other dietary sources, without any competition from excessive polyunsaturated omega-6 fats. Olive oil is also rich in antioxidants, which have many health benefits. Olive oil can be used in cooking and is a good choice for salad dressings. Olive oil margarines are also available.

Peanut oil, which is a mild-tasting oil that oxidizes slowly and can withstand high cooking temperatures. About 50 percent of the fat in peanut oil is monounsaturated and another 30 percent is polyunsaturated. This heart-healthy fat is suitable for Asian cooking such as stir-fries.

Canola oil, which contains significant amounts of omega-3 fat, besides being high in monounsaturated fat. It's a multipurpose cooking oil and can also be used for baking cakes and muffins. Margarine made from canola oil is also available.

Flaxseed (linseed) oil, which is the richest plant source of omega-3s and contains very little omega-6 fat. However, it is highly prone to oxidation (meaning the fats it contains turn rancid easily), so it shouldn't be heated and needs to be stored carefully. It is best used in salad dressings. Alternatively, flaxseeds (linseeds) can be freshly ground and sprinkled on cereals or added to cakes and muffins.

What Fat Is That?

ALTHOUGH FOODS CONTAIN a mixture of fatty acids, one type tends to predominate, allowing us to categorize foods according to their main fatty acid component. The asterisk (*) beside the foods listed below means the food is a good source of omega-3 fatty acids.

POLYUNSATURATED PRODUCTS

Oils—Safflower, sunflower, grapeseed, soybean*, corn, flaxseed* (linseed), cottonseed, walnut*, sesame, evening primrose oils

Spreads—polyunsaturated margarines, tahini (sesame seed paste)

Nuts and seeds—walnuts*, sunflower seeds, pumpkin seeds, sesame seeds

Other plant sources—soybeans, soy milk, whole grains

Animal sources—oily fish*

MONOUNSATURATED PRODUCTS

Oils—olive, canola*, peanut, macadamia, mustard seed oils

Spreads—olive oil margarines, canola margarine*, peanut butter

Nuts and seeds—cashews, macadamias, almonds, hazelnuts, pecans, pistachios, peanuts

Other plant sources—avocado, olives

Animal sources—very lean red meat, lean chicken, lean pork, egg yolks

SATURATED PRODUCTS

Oils/fats—palm and palm kernel oil, coconut oil, drippings, lard, copha, ghee, solid frying oils, cooking margarines, shortening

Spreads—butter, cream cheese

Dairy foods—full-fat dairy products: cheese, cream, sour cream, yogurt, whole milk, ice cream

Animal sources—fat on beef and lamb, skin on chicken, sausage, salami, most luncheon meats

WHAT TO DRINK?

An adequate fluid intake is essential for good health, but most people don't drink enough. Most adults need about 2 liters of fluid each day (about eight 8-ounce glasses) to replace the fluid that is lost from the body. More is needed in hot weather, during exercise, or if you work in air conditioning. An adequate fluid intake is important for kidney function, temperature regulation, and for prevention of constipation.

Water is the best fluid to quench your thirst and is the best choice if you are watching your weight and blood glucose or insulin levels. Soft drinks, energy drinks, and fruit punches contain large amounts of added sugar and it is best to avoid these where possible. Most fruit juices have a relatively low GI and can be consumed in moderation, but remember that they still contain a lot of carbohydrates from the natural fruit sugars. It would be better to eat the whole fruit (which still contains the fiber) rather than drinking the juice.

If you struggle to drink plain water, you could try mineral or soda water with a slice of lemon or lime and a few fresh mint leaves. Or try diluting fruit juice with water, soda water, or mineral water. Tea is also acceptable. Green tea, in particular, has been shown to be high in antioxidants and may have many health benefits. If you like hot drinks, a wide variety of herbal teas is available, but if you are pregnant you need to be careful, because some types are not suitable during pregnancy—check the label.

Coffee and alcohol have a diuretic effect, so they should not be counted as part of your eight glasses. Both are best consumed in moderation. Alcohol is also high in calories, so it should be limited when watching your weight. The recommendations are two to three standard drinks per day for men and one to two for women, with a few alcohol-free days per week. Beer contains gluten and should be avoided on a gluten-free diet, although some gluten-free varieties are now available.

Milk and soy milk are low GI, and the low-fat varieties are the best choice for adults and older children. Full-fat varieties should be given to children up to two years of age. If you don't like the taste of milk or soy milk on its own, you could add a teaspoon of gluten-free drinking chocolate for flavor, or make a fruit smoothie for a satisfying snack or breakfast on the run.

THIS FOR THAT

The bread and cereal group is where most of your decisions about GI need to be made. You may feel like your food choices are already restricted within this food group. But there are plenty of options available, and changing to a low-GI way of eating is often just a matter of swapping one food for another, as shown in the table below. You may actually find that you get more variety in your diet by choosing low GI.

Low-GI Gluten-free Baking

Q: *I'm an avid cook. If I make my own gluten-free bread (or dumplings, pancakes, muffins, etc.), which flours, if any, are gluten-free and low GI?*

A: To date there are no GI ratings for refined flour, whether it's made from rice, legumes, or other gluten-free grains. This is because the GI rating of a food must be tested physiologically—that is, in real people. So far we haven't had volunteers willing to dig in to 1.8-ounce portions of flour on three occasions! What we do know, however, is that bakery products such as bread, cakes, cookies, and muffins made from refined flour, whether it's from rice, maize, buckwheat, or other grains, are quickly digested and absorbed.

continued

continued from page 61

What should you do with your own baking? Try to increase the soluble fiber content by partially substituting rice or maize flour with legume flours (such as soy or chickpea flour—also known as besan) and increase the bulkiness of the product with dried fruit, nuts, seeds, and psyllium husks. Don't think of it as a challenge. It's an opportunity for some creative cooking.

Substituting Low-GI for High-GI Foods

HIGH-GI FOOD	LOW-GI ALTERNATIVE
Bread—most gluten-free varieties	Choose those with whole-kernel grains, legume flours (such as chickpea or soy flour), or psyllium husks and those labeled as "low GI"
Processed breakfast cereals made from puffed or flaked corn and rice	Gluten-free cereals containing rice bran and psyllium
Rice porridge	Quinoa porridge
Corn and rice crackers and crispbreads	Raw nut and seed mixes, roasted chickpeas or soybeans (chick nuts or soy nuts), hummus dip with vegetable crudités
Gluten-free cakes and muffins	Make these with fruit, dried fruits, nuts, seeds, psyllium husks, or rice bran
Potatoes	Baby new potatoes, sweet potatoes, sweet corn, taros, yams, and chestnuts
Rice	Longer grain varieties such as basmati or Uncle Ben's Converted Long-Grain White Rice, or Asian rice noodles
Gluten-free pasta	Lower-GI varieties if available, or Asian rice noodles/vermicelli, buckwheat (soba) noodles, or mung bean (bean thread) noodles

What to Choose When Eating Out

Eating out on a gluten-free diet can be difficult, particularly because items such as sauces, stock, dressings, and gravy often contain gluten. It is important that the restaurant understands your need for a meal that is completely free of gluten, and it may be a good idea to call beforehand to ensure that they can accommodate your needs.

Your local celiac support group should be able to give you a list of recommended restaurants, where you can be confident that they are able to provide you with a gluten-free meal. These are good places to start. Otherwise you need to ask plenty of questions and remember that, if you are in doubt, you are best to leave it out!

Following are some tips to making low-GI gluten-free meal choices when eating out. It will vary from restaurant to restaurant, and it is always important to ask questions.

- Plain grilled steak, chicken, or fish with an ear of sweet corn, and salad or steamed vegetables
- Indian dahl with basmati rice
- Mexican tacos (if 100 percent corn shells) with beans, salad, avocado, salsa, and grated cheese
- Sushi filled with raw fish or avocado and cucumber (no soy sauce)
- Vietnamese rice paper rolls (but hold the dipping sauce unless you can check if it is gluten-free)
- Asian rice noodles stir-fried with vegetables, tofu, or shrimp, peanuts, cilantro, and lemon or lime juice (check the sauces)
- Mixed-bean, chickpea, or lentil salads (leave the dressing unless you can check it is gluten-free)
- Falafel (check that they are gluten-free) with hummus and salad

▪ 6 ▪

Putting the GI to Work
in Your Day

*T*his chapter contains four healthy seven-day menus for
adults, adult vegetarians, teens, and schoolchildren with
an emphasis on low-GI carbs, lean protein, plenty of fruits and
vegetables, and the good oils. We have included recipes from
Part 3 (marked with an asterisk) to inspire you.

The adult menus don't include snacks, but we have suggested some for teenagers and schoolchildren. The teenagers' and
children's menus also reflect different taste preferences and
energy needs during this vital time of growth and development.

Seven-day Menu:
Adult

	BREAKFAST	LUNCH	DINNER
Monday	Creamy Muesli with Mixed Berries*	Individual Spanish Tortilla* with salad Fresh fruit	Grilled Lemon Chicken Skewers with Bean and Asparagus Pilaf* Fruit yogurt
Tuesday	Whole-grain gluten-free toast with baked beans	Gluten-free wrap with chicken breast, avocado, and salad	Salmon and Squash Patties with Lima Bean Salad* Garden salad Low-fat gluten-free hot chocolate
Wednesday	Peachy Pistachio Porridge*	Chicken Pasta Salad with Mango Salsa* Dried-fruit and nut mix	Greek-style Beef Skewers* Fresh fruit salad with yogurt
Thursday	Turkey, Avocado, & Fresh Peach Salsa Wrap*	Velvety Squash Soup* Fresh fruit	Lamb Curry with Spinach Rice Pilaf* Berry Yogurt Delight*
Friday	Seriously Strawberry Smoothie*	Warm Potato Salad with Herbs and Toasted Hazelnuts* Fresh fruit	Pork, Bok Choy, and Noodle Stir-fry* Low-fat gluten-free hot chocolate
Saturday	Breakfast Fried Rice*	Tuna Pasta Niçoise* Fruit yogurt	Cranberry Chicken with Quinoa* Green beans and carrots Berry-Pear Cobbler*
Sunday	Gluten-free toast with scrambled eggs and grilled tomatoes	Thai Beef Salad with Chili Lime Dressing* Fresh fruit	Herb Fish Packets with Fennel, Bean, and Tomato Salad* Rhubarb and Apple Crumble* with reduced-fat gluten-free pudding

Seven-day Menu:
Adult Vegetarian

	BREAKFAST	LUNCH	DINNER
Monday	Gluten-free Granola with Pecans and Almonds* with low-fat milk or gluten-free soy milk	Carrot, Avocado, and Snow Pea Rice Paper Rolls* Fresh fruit	Vegetarian Pad Thai* Fruit yogurt
Tuesday	Whole-grain gluten-free toast with baked beans	Chunky Tomato Soup with Chickpeas* Dried-fruit and nut mix	Spinach Rice Pilaf* (see Lamb Curry with Spinach Rice Pilaf) with pine nuts Gluten-free hot chocolate
Wednesday	Peachy Pistachio Porridge*	Warm Potato Salad with Herbs and Toasted Hazelnuts* Fresh fruit	Tofu Laksa* (see Shrimp Laksa— variation) Cranberry Baked Apple* with low-fat yogurt
Thursday	Whole-grain gluten-free toast with avocado and tomato	Avocado and Tofu Sushi* Fresh fruit	Squash, Ricotta, and Lentil Lasagna* Gluten-free hot chocolate
Friday	Banana and Passion Fruit Smoothie*	Gluten-free pasta salad tossed with roasted butternut squash, chickpeas, and pine nuts Fresh fruit	Tofu, Bok Choy, and Rice Noodle Stir-fry* (Pork, Bok Choy, and Rice Noodle Stir-fry variation) Fruit salad with low-fat yogurt
Saturday	Multigrain Porridge with Apple*	Lentil and Feta Salad* Dried-fruit and nut mix	Falafel* with Pistachio and Quinoa Tabbouleh*, and Hummus* Chocolate Almond Cake* with reduced-fat gluten-free pudding
Sunday	Tofu Pancakes with Avocado, Tomato, and Corn Salsa*	Velvety Squash Soup* Fresh fruit	Chili Bean Tacos* Rhubarb and Apple Crumble* with reduced-fat gluten-free pudding

Note: Choose soy products (milk, custard, yogurt) fortified with vitamin B_{12} where possible, or take a vitamin B_{12} supplement.

Seven-day Menu:
Teenager

	BREAKFAST	LUNCH	DINNER
Monday	Multigrain Porridge with Apple* Glass of fruit juice SNACK: Dried-fruit and nut mix and a banana	Gluten-free wrap with turkey, avocado, and salad Fresh fruit SNACK: Fruit yogurt	Salmon and Squash Patties* with peas and beans Chocolate Mousse*
Tuesday	Ricotta, Strawberry, and Banana Wrap* Glass of milk SNACK: Apple plus gluten-free crackers and cheese	Chicken Pasta with Mango Salsa* Fresh fruit SNACK: Fruit Loaf* with gluten-free hot chocolate	Homemade gluten-free pizza Berry-Pear Cobbler*
Wednesday	Creamy Muesli with Mixed Berries* SNACK: Apple and Pecan Muffin*	Individual Spanish Tortilla* SNACK: Gluten-free toast with peanut butter	Chicken Tacos* Fruit salad with yogurt
Thursday	Whole-grain gluten-free toast with peanut butter Gluten-free hot chocolate SNACK: Banana plus Apricot Nut Slice*	Easy Tuna Bake* with cherry tomatoes Dried-fruit and nut mix SNACK: Fruit yogurt	Pork, Bok Choy, and Rice Noodle Stir-fry* Gluten-free hot chocolate
Friday	Banana and Passion Fruit Smoothie* SNACK: Rice cakes with peanut butter	Sushi with Salmon* SNACK: Muesli Nut Cookie* plus glass of milk	Pasta with Italian Meatballs in Tomato Sauce* and salad Rhubarb and Apple Crumble* with reduced-fat ice cream
Saturday	Apricot and Strawberry Parfait Crunch* SNACK: Apple plus dried-fruit and nut mix	Chicken Nuggets with Salad* Fresh fruit SNACK: Fruit smoothie	Thai Beef Salad with Chili Lime Dressing* Honey Banana Cups with Lime and Coconut Macaroons*
Sunday	Whole-grain gluten-free toasted sandwich with baked beans and cheese SNACK: Apple	Rice Paper Rolls* SNACK: Cheese and gluten-free crackers	Beef and Bean Fajitas* Berry Yogurt Delight*

Seven-day Menu:
Schoolchild

	BREAKFAST	LUNCH	DINNER
Monday	Fresh fruit combo with yogurt SNACK: Small box of raisins	Gluten-free wrap with ham, cheese, and pineapple Fruit salad SNACK: Fruit yogurt	Easy Chicken and Corn Soup* with gluten-free toast Berry Yogurt Delight* (served in parfait glass)
Tuesday	Ricotta, Strawberry, and Banana Wrap* SNACK: Apple	Rice Paper Rolls* SNACK: Fruit Loaf* with gluten-free hot chocolate	Shepherd's pie with carrots and peas Banana split
Wednesday	Gluten-free cereal with milk and sliced peaches SNACK: Handful of dried fruit	Chicken Nuggets with Salad* SNACK: Gluten-free toast with peanut butter	Homemade fried rice Yogurt Strawberry Jell-O*
Thursday	Whole-grain gluten-free toast with baked beans SNACK: Grapes	Individual Spanish Tortilla* Small box of raisins SNACK: Fruit pieces with yogurt dip	Chicken Tacos* Chocolate Mousse*
Friday	Seriously Strawberry Smoothie* SNACK: Gluten-free crackers with peanut butter	Gluten-free wrap with peanut butter, raisins and grated carrot Kiwi fruit SNACK: Brownie*	Easy Tuna Bake* with salad Rhubarb and Apple Crumble* with ice cream
Saturday	Breakfast Fried Rice* SNACK: Orange	Baked bean gluten-free whole-grain toasted sandwich SNACK: Raisins and glass of milk	Chicken and Rice Lettuce Cups* Passion Fruit Banana Cups* with Lime and Coconut Macaroons*
Sunday	Gluten-free toast with scrambled egg SNACK: Apple	Gluten-free homemade pizza SNACK: Banana and Passion Fruit Smoothie*	Spaghetti with Italian Meatballs in Tomato Sauce* Frozen fruit kebabs

PART 3

Eat Yourself Healthy

Recipes with a healthy balance for breakfast, lunch, dinner, desserts, and snacks. Plus plenty of options for the school lunchbox.

COOKING THE LOW-GI WAY

One of the aims of our books is to show you easy ways to lower the GI of your diet. For those who like to cook, low- (or lower) GI recipes are part of the picture. Even if you don't like the following recipes, you will find that they give you ideas of how you can use low-GI ingredients in flavorful and nutritious combinations.

Naturally we aim to develop recipes with as low a GI as possible, and most of the recipes in this book are low GI, but there are a few popular dishes for which even we find this difficult! Typically these are baked goods made with flour, such as muffins and cakes. Because flour is a finely milled product, it is rapidly digested and has a high GI. By incorporating lower-GI carbs and lots of fiber such as whole-kernel grains, rice bran, psyllium husks, fruit, milk, and juices into these recipes, we can lower the GI.

Modern diets contain much more sodium (salt) than is commensurate with good health, so one of our guidelines when creating recipes is to limit sodium intake. We don't add salt to our cooking and we use reduced-salt gluten-free products where possible. You may think cutting salt will be difficult but your taste buds will adapt pretty quickly. You can add flavor to your meals by using herbs and spices, lemon juice, and pepper. You may like to invest in a good pepper grinder!

NUTRIENT PROFILE

Each recipe is accompanied by a nutrient profile,[1] which gives you a snapshot of its key nutritional attributes. The profile

---

[1] Recipes have been analyzed using nutrient analysis software, FoodWorks (Xyris Software), based on Australian and New Zealand food composition data.

normally relates to a single serving assuming you divide the recipe to make the specified number of servings, or to one item for wraps, tacos, fajitas, muffins, cookies, etc. If you eat a double or triple serving of the recipe, then you would scale up the figures two or three times, respectively.

In the nutrient profile for the recipes, we include calories, fat (including saturated fat), fiber, protein, and carbohydrates.

Calories

The smaller the number, the fewer the calories (or fuel) in a serving. This is a good thing if you have a tendency to gain weight. By incorporating lots of vegetables, salads, fruits, and whole-kernel grains into the recipes, we have ensured that many have a low energy density. This means that they are bulky and filling without providing lots of calories.

Fat

The fat content is given in grams per serving (or item). This is useful if you are trying to eat a low-fat diet. If the figure seems a little high on some recipes, rest assured it is mostly "good" fat or of a poly- or monounsaturated nature. A low saturated-fat intake is recommended for everyone, and all our recipes are low in saturated fat.

Fiber

Experts recommend a daily fiber intake of 30 grams, but most people fall short of that, averaging 20 to 25 grams. And it can be more difficult to get enough fiber on a gluten-free diet due to the absence of many grain foods. You'll find that most of our recipes are fiber-rich. This means they'll not only keep you regular but also will help lower your blood glucose and cholesterol levels and reduce your risk of many chronic diseases.

Protein

The protein content is given in grams per serving. Most of us get plenty of protein without having to think about it. Sufficient protein in the diet is important for weight control because compared with carbohydrates and fats, protein makes us feel more satisfied immediately after eating and reduces hunger between meals. Protein also increases our metabolic rate for one to three hours after eating. This means we burn more energy by the minute compared with the increase that occurs after eating carbohydrates or fats. Even though this is a relatively small difference, it may be important in long-term weight control.

Carbohydrates

The amount of carbohydrates per serving in grams may be of most interest to those with diabetes. Because the GI relates only to the carbohydrate content of foods, you will find that most of our recipes have a significant carbohydrate content.

CONVERSIONS

Dry measurements	
IMPERIAL	METRIC
½ oz	15 g
1 oz	30 g
1½ oz	45 g
2 oz	55 g
4 oz	115 g
5 oz	150 g
6½ oz	180 g
7 oz	200 g
8 oz	230 g
1 lb 2 oz	500 g
2 lb	1 kg

Liquid measurements

IMPERIAL	STANDARD CUPS	METRIC
1 fl oz	2 tbsp	30 ml
2 fl oz	¼ cup	60 ml
2¾ fl oz	⅓ cup	80 ml
4 fl oz	½ cup	125 ml
6 fl oz	¾ cup	185 ml
8 fl oz	1 cup	250 ml

Temperatures

FAHRENHEIT	CELSIUS
250°F	120°C
300°F	150°C
315°F	160°C
350°F	180°C
375°F	190°C
400°F	200°C
425°F	220°C
450°F	230°C
475°F	240°C

INGREDIENTS

Breadcrumbs

To make fresh gluten-free breadcrumbs:

- Tear slices of gluten-free bread, including the crusts, into 3 or 4 pieces and process in a food processor. It's a good idea to make extra breadcrumbs while you have the processor running and freeze the rest in 1-cup quantities. They will defrost very quickly when you need to use them. Store in an airtight plastic container (a zip-lock bag would be fine) in the freezer for up to 2 months.

- 1 slice of bread makes about ⅓ cup. If you don't have a food processor, use a coarse grater.

To make dried gluten-free breadcrumbs:

- Preheat the oven to 350°F. Cut the bread into 4 squares. Lay squares on a wire rack and place in a baking dish. Bake for 10–15 minutes or until just colored. Turn off the oven and leave bread there for 20–25 minutes or until bread is hard. Break the bread into smaller pieces and process in a food processor until crumbed.
- 2 slices of bread make about ½ cup dried breadcrumbs. If you don't have a food processor, put the bread in a strong plastic bag and crush with a rolling pin.

Eggs

We use large eggs in our recipes.

Flour

In our recipes we use a variety of gluten-free flours, including rice flour, brown rice flour, besan (chickpea flour), buckwheat flour, cornstarch, and potato flour. You'll find these in larger supermarkets and health food stores. When buying cornstarch, make sure you get the gluten-free variety (made from corn), because regular cornstarch is not actually corn but fine wheat flour. Make sure you buy gluten-free baking powder, too.

Margarine

We used reduced-fat poly- or monounsaturated-fat margarines in our cooking.

Pasta

As we explained earlier, many gluten-free pastas made from rice or corn have a high GI. That's why we combine pasta with lots of low-GI ingredients in our recipes. Soy pastas may be lower-GI than those made from corn or rice flour.

Rice

We use lower-GI rices in our recipes and as serving suggestions—basmati (GI 58) and Uncle Ben's Converted Long-Grain White Rice (GI 45).

Spices

A number of recipes have premixed herb and spice blends. We like the Gourmet du Village brand because the quality and flavor are outstanding and, except for asafetida and blends containing asafetida, they are all gluten-free. Check all labels on supermarket brands carefully for gluten content and if you're unsure, see page 246 for more information on how to buy the Gourmet du Village range. Always check the labels when buying spice blends, because some may contain gluten.

Stock

If you don't have time to make your own stock, check that the one you buy is gluten-free and reduced-salt. Swanson is a good brand to look for and is widely available in supermarkets. Be sure to check the label, because not all of their broths are gluten-free.

Tamari

You can buy tamari from Asian produce stores and the Asian section of supermarkets. Gluten-free tamari is one of the authentic soy sauce recipes first introduced to Japan from China. It is a wheat-free sauce made from soybeans and has a slightly stronger flavor than regular soy sauce. It's traditionally used to flavor longer-cooking foods (soups, stews, etc.), but it can be used in marinades and dressings too, or as a condiment or dipping sauce. Look for reduced-salt tamari.

Xanthan Gum

You'll find this handy ingredient in health food stores or the health food aisle of major supermarkets. It's widely used in gluten-free baking to improve the texture of the final product. It's more expensive than baking powder, but a small pouch goes a long way.

ALL TEASPOON, TABLESPOON, and cup measurements are level.

·7·

Breakfasts and Brunches

A **healthy breakfast** that includes gluten-free whole grains and fruit is a great start in meeting your daily fiber intake. Nourish your body, recharge your brain, boost your metabolism, and power your day with our tasty breakfasts and brunches.

GI EXPRESS: BREAKFAST BASICS

Hot!

CEREAL PLUS

1. **Start** with a bowl of steaming quinoa porridge (made with whole grains, not flakes).
2. **Add** lots of fresh or frozen berries, stirring them in gently.
3. **Top** with a dollop of low-fat plain yogurt and a sprinkling of sugar.

TOAST PLUS

1. **Start** by toasting gluten-free bread.
2. **Add** 2–3 tablespoons of creamed corn and spread it over evenly.
3. **Top** with fresh mushroom slices, a slice or two of tomato, and a sprinkle of part-skim mozzarella cheese. Grill until the cheese melts and the corn is bubbly.

Cold!

CEREAL PLUS

1. **Start** with your favorite gluten-free muesli.
2. **Add** low-fat milk and fresh slices of apple or pear; ½ cup sliced strawberries, blueberries, or orange segments; or ½ banana, sliced.
3. **Top** with a dollop of plain or flavored low-fat yogurt and a sprinkle of chopped nuts.

TOAST PLUS

1. **Start** by toasting gluten-free bread.
2. **Add** 2–3 tablespoons of fresh ricotta and spread it evenly.
3. **Top** with a dollop of all-fruit spread such as apricot or strawberry, or a drizzle of pure floral honey.

SEE PAGE 29 for guidelines about choosing gluten-free breads and breakfast cereals with a lower GI.

CREAMY MUESLI WITH BERRIES

*T*his recipe makes a thick muesli. If you prefer a "runnier" texture, add extra milk before serving. The textures of brown rice flakes vary considerably among brands. Some are actually a breakfast-cereal flake like cornflakes. Look for smaller, denser, heavier flakes to use as an ingredient. The brand we used in our cooking weighed in at 1¾ ounces per half cup.

SERVES 1 ■ SOAKING TIME Overnight ■ **PREPARATION TIME 5 minutes**

⅓ cup brown rice flakes
2 teaspoons rice bran
⅓ cup low-fat milk or soy milk
½ apple, grated with skin on
1 teaspoon psyllium husks

To Serve
¼ cup blueberries or sliced strawberries
1½ tablespoons low-fat plain yogurt or soy yogurt
1½ tablespoons slivered almonds, lightly toasted

1. The night before, place the rice flakes, rice bran, and milk in a bowl. Cover and leave in the refrigerator overnight.
2. In the morning, stir in the grated apple and psyllium husks and top with berries, a dollop or two of yogurt, and the slivered, toasted almonds.

VARIATIONS
- Replace the milk with orange juice.
- Replace the almonds with chopped walnuts—they don't need toasting.
- Replace the berries with your favorite fruit, such as ½ banana, sliced; pulp of 1–2 passion fruit; canned (in water or natural juice) peach or pear slices; apricot halves; or 1–2 plums.

◄ PER SERVING ►
310 cal; 8 g fat (including 1.5 g saturated fat); 7 g fiber;
10 g protein; 45 g carbohydrates

GLUTEN-FREE GRANOLA
WITH PECANS AND ALMONDS

*I*t doesn't quite snap, crackle, and pop—but it comes pretty close. The secret is in the slow cooking. You don't have to worry about it burning as it gently toasts to a golden brown in a low oven. After you have made the recipe a couple of times, mix and match the ingredients to suit your family's likes and dislikes. The granola can be stored in a cool cupboard for up to 10 days.

MAKES about 8 cups ■ **PREPARATION TIME** 15 minutes ■
COOKING TIME 30 minutes

---

1 cup brown puffed rice
1 cup puffed buckwheat
1 cup puffed millet
½ cup quinoa flakes
½ cup brown rice flakes
¼ cup rice bran
1 cup roughly chopped pecans
1 cup slivered almonds
½ cup pumpkin seeds
½ cup sunflower seeds
2½ tablespoons walnut or canola oil
¼ cup pure floral honey
1 cup dried cranberries (or raisins or currants)

1. Preheat the oven to 300°F.
2. Combine the grains, nuts, and seeds in a large bowl and mix together well.
3. In a small saucepan, blend the oil and honey, and cook over low heat until just melted.
4. Stir the syrup mixture into the bowl of muesli until the ingredients are lightly coated.
5. Spread evenly over a large, rimmed baking sheet. Bake for 30 minutes, stirring halfway through to toast evenly, or until gold-

en brown. Cool completely on the tray, then add the dried fruit. Spoon into a large airtight container.

6. Serve ½ cup granola with ¼ cup milk and 1 tablespoon yogurt.

VARIATIONS
- Add chopped dates, figs, quartered figs, or sliced apricots.
- For a tangy change, moisten with a little sour cherry or pomegranate juice.

◄ **PER SERVING INCLUDING MILK AND YOGURT** ►
288 cal; 17 g fat (including 2 g saturated fat); 3 g fiber;
9 g protein; 25 g carbohydrates

BANANA AND PASSION FRUIT SMOOTHIE

$\mathcal{F}$or a really delicious smoothie, the trick is to make sure the milk is very cold. Freeze leftovers for after-school ice pops on hot days.

SERVES 2 ■ PREPARATION TIME 5 minutes

---

1 medium banana, chopped
1 cup low-fat milk or light gluten-free soy milk, chilled
1 container (6-ounce) low-fat passion fruit yogurt or gluten-free soy yogurt
2 teaspoons rice bran
2 teaspoons pure floral honey (optional)

1. Combine all the ingredients in a blender and blend until smooth. Pour into two tall glasses and serve.

◄ PER SERVING ►
215 cal; 2 g fat (including 1.5 g saturated fat); 1.5 g fiber;
11 g protein; 36 g carbohydrates

Bananas

BANANAS ARE NOT only fat-free and high in dietary fiber, but they also are a good source of carbohydrates for energy. They also provide potassium and are high in vitamin B_6. Firm bananas have a low GI, but this increases as they ripen, as some of the starches change into sugars.

Bananas make the ideal portable snack but can also be used in cakes, muffins, pancakes, smoothies, and desserts such as puddings, soufflés, and the good old banana split!

CHERIMOYA AND ORANGE SMOOTHIE

*C*herimoyas (custard apples) are in season from May to November. So, you have serveral months to make the most of this creamy fruit that tastes like a tropical fruit salad and is a good source of carbs, protein, fiber, and essential vitamins and minerals.

SERVES 2 ■ PREPARATION TIME 5 minutes

---

1 cup cherimoya pulp
½ cup low-fat milk or light gluten-free soy milk, chilled
½ cup orange juice
1 container (6 ounces) low-fat vanilla yogurt or gluten-free soy yogurt
2 teaspoons rice bran
2 teaspoons pure floral honey (optional)

1. Combine all the ingredients in a blender and blend until smooth. Pour into two tall glasses and serve.

◄ PER SERVING ►
259 cal; 2.5 g fat (including 1 g saturated fat); 4 g fiber;
11 g protein; 47 g carbohydrates

Cherimoya

DON'T BE PUT off by its green, bumpy skin—a **cherimoya** tastes rather like a tropical fruit salad all in one fruit! The ripe ones give slightly when you squeeze them gently, much like avocados. Simply cut in half and scoop out the white flesh. You can eat them raw, add to fruit salads or mashed bananas, make into ice creams and sorbets, or use in drinks, desserts, fillings for cakes, and as an accompaniment to spicy dishes such as curry. Serve cut wedges on a fruit and cheese platter, but brush them with a little lemon juice first to prevent discoloring.

SERIOUSLY STRAWBERRY SMOOTHIE

*Y*ou can make this with any berry-flavored yogurt—or with any mixture of berries, for that matter.

SERVES 2 ■ PREPARATION TIME 5 minutes

---

1 pint strawberries, hulled
1 cup low-fat milk or light gluten-free soy milk, chilled
1 tub (6 ounces) low-fat strawberry yogurt or gluten-free soy yogurt
2 teaspoons rice bran
2 teaspoons pure floral honey (optional)

1. Combine all the ingredients in a blender and blend until smooth. Pour into two tall glasses and serve.

◄ **PER SERVING** ►
193 cal; 2 g fat (including 1.5 g saturated fat); 2.5 g fiber;
12 g protein; 29 g carbohydrates

Berries

BERRIES ARE A great source of folate, vitamin C, and antioxidants, which can protect the body against the effects of aging and a range of degenerative diseases. Berries have also been shown to display anticancer properties, and cranberries can help reduce the risk of urinary tract infections.

Versatile and with natural sweetness, berries can be eaten on their own, served with yogurt or ice cream, sliced on top of cereal, added to fruit salads, platters, and cheese boards, used in mousses, tarts, muffins, and cakes, or made into jam.

APRICOT AND STRAWBERRY PARFAIT CRUNCH

*T*empt those sleepyheads and breakfast-skippers with a parfait treat. We leave the skin on the apricots, but you can peel them (as you would peel tomatoes) if you prefer. In the cooler months, when fresh apricots aren't in season, this smoothie is delicious made with apricot compote (made with dried apricots) or even with canned (in water or natural juice) apricot halves. For the mixed nuts, choose from almonds, walnuts, pistachios, hazelnuts, Brazil nuts, and cashews.

SERVES 4 ■ PREPARATION TIME 10 minutes ■ COOKING TIME 1–2 minutes

---

⅓ cup mixed raw nuts
¼ cup sunflower seeds
¼ cup pumpkin seeds
8 fresh apricots, washed
2½ cups low-fat vanilla yogurt
1 pint strawberries, sliced (or other berries in season)

1. Heat a nonstick frying pan over medium heat and add the nuts and seeds. Toast gently for 1–2 minutes, stirring continuously, or until just golden brown (take care, as nuts burn very quickly). Remove from the heat and spread nuts on a paper towel. When cool enough to handle, chop roughly.
2. Halve the apricots, remove the pits, and cut each half into 2–3 slices.
3. Take 4 tall glasses and spoon a little yogurt into the bottom of each one. Divide the apricot slices among the glasses, top with another layer of yogurt, then finish with a layer of strawberries. Top with a good sprinkle of the crunchy toasted nut and seed mixture.

◄ PER SERVING ►
343 cal; 15 g fat (including 1.5 g saturated fat); 6 g fiber;
16 g protein; 31 g carbohydrates

PEACHY PISTACHIO PORRIDGE

*P*eaches (poached or canned) and pistachios make a great combo with creamy quinoa porridge. Use peaches canned in water or natural juice.

SERVES 4 ■ PREPARATION TIME 10 minutes ■ COOKING TIME 15 minutes

1 cup quinoa, rinsed
2 cups low-fat milk or gluten-free soy milk
1 apple, chopped with skin on
1 cinnamon stick or ½ teaspoon ground cinnamon
2 teaspoons psyllium husks

To Serve
4 poached or canned peach halves
⅓ cup low-fat vanilla yogurt
¼ cup finely chopped pistachios
1 cup low-fat milk or gluten-free soy milk

1. Combine the rinsed quinoa with the milk in a saucepan. Bring to a boil over medium heat (make sure that the milk doesn't boil over), then reduce the heat to low and simmer gently, stirring occasionally, for 5 minutes. Add the apple and cinnamon and simmer for 5–6 minutes, or until all liquid is absorbed and porridge is creamy. Remove the cinnamon stick, if using. Stir in the psyllium husks.

2. Spoon the porridge into breakfast bowls and serve topped with peach halves or slices, a tablespoon of yogurt, a sprinkle of pistachios, and a little milk.

VARIATIONS
- Try poached or canned plums for a tangy change.
- Chopped walnuts or lightly toasted almond slivers make a crunchy topping.

◄ PER SERVING ►
396 cal; 9 g fat (including 2 g saturated fat); 7.5 g fiber;
17 g protein; 57 g carbohydrates

MULTIGRAIN PORRIDGE WITH APPLE

*T*here's nothing better on a cold morning than a warm breakfast. Enjoy this combination of grains and nuts as is or, if you wish, add a tablespoon or two of raisins for extra texture. We like using cloudy apple juice because research shows it has almost four times more antioxidants than clear juice. And it's naturally sweet, so you don't need to top the porridge with extra sugar or honey.

SERVES 4 ■ PREPARATION TIME 5 minutes ■ COOKING TIME 5 minutes

---

⅓ cup quinoa flakes
⅓ cup brown rice flakes
½ teaspoon ground cinnamon
1½ tablespoons rice bran
2½ cups cloudy apple juice
2 teaspoons psyllium husks
¼ cup finely chopped mixed nuts (almonds, cashews, Brazil nuts, macadamias, hazelnuts, walnuts)

To Serve
1 cup low-fat milk or gluten-free soy milk
⅓ cup low-fat plain or flavored yogurt (optional)

1. Place the quinoa flakes, rice flakes, cinnamon, rice bran, and juice in a saucepan, and bring to a boil over medium heat. Reduce the heat to low and simmer gently for 2–3 minutes, stirring occasionally, or until the liquid is absorbed and you have a creamy porridge.

2. Remove from heat and stir in the psyllium husks and finely chopped nuts. Spoon the porridge into breakfast bowls and serve with milk and a tablespoon of yogurt.

◄ PER SERVING ►
265 cal; 7 g fat (including 1.5 g saturated fat); 3.5 g fiber;
8 g protein; 42 g carbohydrates

RICOTTA, STRAWBERRY, AND BANANA WRAPS

*K*ate's favorite flatbread is Gluten Free Organic Tannour Bread—it's delicious but, sadly, not widely available. Look for it in organic or health food stores. A growing number of gluten-free flatbreads are available in supermarkets, but they have no published GI values yet. So make sure your fillings include low-GI ingredients.

MAKES 2 ■ PREPARATION TIME 5 minutes

3½ ounces reduced-fat ricotta or cottage cheese
2 sheets gluten-free flatbread
1 medium banana, sliced
½ cup finely sliced strawberries

1. Spread the ricotta over two-thirds of each flatbread and top with banana and strawberry slices. Wrap to enclose the filling and serve.

◄ PER WRAP ►
262 cal; 7 g fat (including 3 g saturated fat); 2.5 g fiber;
8 g protein; 40 g carbohydrates

TURKEY, AVOCADO, AND FRESH PEACH SALSA WRAPS

MAKES 2 ■ PREPARATION TIME 15 minutes

4 iceberg lettuce leaves, roughly shredded
2 sheets gluten-free flatbread
4 gluten-free turkey slices
½ avocado, peeled, pit removed, and finely sliced

Fresh Peach Salsa

1 peach, peeled and chopped
½ Lebanese cucumber, chopped
2 teaspoons chopped mint
1 scallion, finely sliced

1. To make the salsa, combine all ingredients in a bowl. Set aside.

2. Spread the shredded lettuce over ⅔ of each flatbread and top each with 2 turkey slices and 2 avocado slices.

3. Spoon the Fresh Peach Salsa over the turkey and roll up to enclose the filling. If not serving immediately, wrap in paper or foil and store in the refrigerator for up to 5 hours.

VARIATION
■ Replace the peach salsa with a tablespoon of cranberry sauce.

◄ PER WRAP ►
372 cal; 18 g fat (including 3.5 g saturated fat); 3 g fiber;
17 g protein; 34 g carbohydrates

TOFU PANCAKES WITH AVOCADO, TOMATO, AND CORN SALSA

*T*hese pancakes are also delicious served with oven-roasted tomatoes or sautéed mushrooms. Keep the cooked pancakes warm on a plate covered with foil in a very low-heat oven, about 250°F, while cooking the remaining batter. Halve the quantities if you want to make only 4.

MAKES 8 ■ **PREPARATION TIME** 15 minutes ■ **COOKING TIME** 40 minutes

---

10 ounces silken tofu, drained
2 eggs
1 cup low-fat gluten-free soy milk
1 cup rice flour
½ cup besan (chickpea) flour
1½ tablespoons gluten-free baking powder
canola oil spray

Avocado, Tomato, and Corn Salsa
1 ear corn (or 1 cup canned or frozen corn kernels)
2 ripe tomatoes, finely chopped
1 small ripe avocado, finely chopped
½ small red (Spanish) onion, finely chopped
1 small red chili, finely chopped
⅓ cup finely chopped cilantro
2½ tablespoons fresh lime juice
1 tablespoon olive oil
freshly ground black pepper

1. Preheat oven to 250°F to keep the pancakes warm once you have made them.
2. To make the salsa, microwave or steam the corn (if using fresh) until just tender. Set aside to cool slightly. Cut the kernels off the cob and place them in a bowl with the tomato, avocado, onion, chili, cilantro, lime juice, and oil. Stir gently, season with pepper, and set aside.
3. To make the pancakes, place the tofu in a bowl and use a fork to mash. Whisk in the eggs and soy milk. Sift the rice flour,

besan, and baking powder into a bowl, add to the tofu mixture, and mix until well combined.

4. Spray a large nonstick frying pan with oil and place over medium heat. Drop ⅓ cup of the batter into the pan and spread out to about a 4-inch diameter. Cook for 3 minutes or until golden underneath. Turn carefully and cook 2 more minutes or until the pancake has risen and is golden brown and cooked through. Repeat with the remaining batter to make 8 pancakes.

5. To serve, place a pancake on each plate and top with the salsa. Cover any leftover salsa and store in the refrigerator for up to 2 days.

VARIATIONS
- For a quicker and easier topping, replace the Avocado, Tomato and Corn Salsa with a 14-ounce can of baked beans combined with creamed corn.
- The salsa can be replaced with oven-roasted tomatoes or sautéed mushrooms.

◄ **PER PANCAKE** ►
336 cal; 16 g fat (including 3 g saturated fat); 5 g fiber;
14 g protein; 32 g carbohydrates

PORTOBELLO PIZZAS
WITH PARMESAN CRUMB

*T*his filling brunch will power you for just about the rest of the day. It's also great served as a light meal.

SERVES 6 ■ PREPARATION TIME 10 minutes ■ COOKING TIME 30 minutes

---

2–3 tablespoons olive oil

6 portobello (or meadow) mushrooms, wiped; remove stems and chop

1 onion, finely chopped

3 cloves garlic, finely chopped

1 small red pepper, finely chopped

14-ounce can diced tomatoes

14-ounce can gluten-free lentils, drained

small bunch basil leaves, washed and torn

freshly ground black pepper

1 cup grated Parmesan cheese

1 cup low-GI gluten-free whole-grain breadcrumbs

To Serve
wilted baby spinach

1. Preheat the oven to 350°F.

2. Grease an oven tray with a little of the olive oil. Brush some oil over the base of the mushrooms and place them on the tray.

3. Heat the remaining oil in a large nonstick frying pan over medium heat. Add the mushroom stems, onion, garlic, and pepper. Reduce the heat and cook, stirring occasionally, for 10 minutes or until the onions are soft and golden. Stir in the diced tomatoes, then add the lentils and basil and stir gently until the mixture is well combined and heated through. Season with pepper and set aside.

4. Process the Parmesan cheese and breadcrumbs to fine crumbs. Spoon the lentil mixture into the mushroom caps and top each one with the breadcrumb mixture.

5. Place tray in the oven and bake for 15 minutes or until the topping is crisp and golden and the mushrooms are cooked through. (Cooking time will vary a little depending on the size of the mushrooms.)

6. Place a little wilted spinach on each plate, top with a mushroom, and serve.

◄ PER SERVING ►
280 cal; 14 g fat (including 4 g saturated fat); 6 g fiber;
14 g protein; 23 g carbohydrates

10 Toast-topper Tips

MANY GLUTEN-FREE breads taste much better toasted. Here are some toppings and fillings that will help power your day:

- Baked beans topped with grated reduced-fat cheese
- Creamed corn topped with lean gluten-free ham
- Scrambled egg with basil
- Sautéed mushrooms with parsley
- Labne (yogurt cheese or Greek yogurt) with cucumber and tomato slices
- Avocado, spinach, and tomato slices
- Ricotta, sliced pears or apples, and chopped walnuts
- Hummus and tomato
- Avocado with canned pinto beans
- Ricotta, sliced plums, and slivered almonds

BREAKFAST FRIED RICE

*W*hen preparing rice for evening meals, cook extra so you have leftovers. This fried rice is also good for the lunchbox. Look for tamari sauce in the Asian section of your supermarket.

SERVES 4 ■ PREPARATION TIME 5 minutes ■ COOKING TIME 10 minutes

---

canola oil spray
2 eggs, at room temperature
1 tablespoon canola oil
1 small red pepper, finely chopped
1 cup frozen corn kernels, thawed
1 cup frozen peas, thawed
3 cups cooked low-GI or basmati rice
3 scallions, finely sliced on the diagonal
2½ tablespoons reduced-salt gluten-free tamari
¼ cup lightly toasted and chopped cashews

1. Heat a large nonstick frying pan or wok over medium heat and use canola oil spray to coat the base (or sides of the wok). Whisk the eggs until frothy, pour into the pan and swirl to cover the base (or sides of the wok). Cook for 2 minutes or until the egg is set. Carefully loosen the edges, turn out onto a large plate, and set aside to cool. Roll up the omelet, cut into thin strips, and set aside.
2. Heat the canola oil in the pan over medium-high heat. Add the pepper, corn, and peas, and cook, tossing gently, for 2 minutes or until heated through. Add the rice and stir-fry for 2–3 minutes or until heated through. Add the sliced omelet, scallions, and tamari sauce, and stir-fry to heat through and combine well.
3. Serve topped with the toasted cashews.

VARIATION
- ■ Replace the corn, peas, and pepper with 3 cups frozen corn, pea, and carrot mix.

◄ PER SERVING ►
390 cal; 14 g fat (including 2 g saturated fat); 5.5 g fiber; 12 g protein;
51 g carbohydrates

▪ 8 ▪

Snacks and Treats

*S*nacks **prevent us** from becoming too hungry and reduce the likelihood of overeating when mealtimes come around. The key is to keep them healthy, quick, and easy to prepare.

APPLE AND PECAN MUFFINS

$\mathcal{L}$ow-GI baking is a challenge, surpassed only by low-GI gluten-free baking! Diane Temple, our recipe tester, will testify to this. Here we boost the fiber and lower the GI with ingredients such as psyllium husks, banana, apple, and brown rice flour. Sifting is the secret of successful gluten-free baking. These muffins remain fresh for a day. Freezing will keep them longer.

**MAKES 12 ■ PREPARATION TIME 25 minutes ■
COOKING TIME 20 minutes + cooling time**

> canola oil spray
> ¾ cup rice flour
> ½ cup brown rice flour
> ½ cup gluten-free cornstarch
> ¼ cup soy flour
> 2 teaspoons gluten-free baking powder
> 1 teaspoon baking soda
> 1 teaspoon xanthan gum
> 1½ tablespoons psyllium husks
> ½ cup superfine sugar
> 1 egg
> 1½ tablespoons canola oil
> 1 teaspoon vanilla extract
> ½ cup reduced-fat milk
> 1 small banana, mashed (about ⅓ cup)
> 1 large green apple, peeled, cored, and diced (about 1 cup)
> ⅓ cup roughly chopped pecans

1. Preheat the oven to 350°F. Coat a 12-hole (each ⅓-cup capacity) muffin pan with canola oil spray.
2. In a large mixing bowl, sift together the rice flour, brown rice flour, cornstarch, soy flour, baking powder, baking soda and xanthan gum. Stir to mix well, then sift a second time into another large bowl. Stir in the psyllium husks and sugar.
3. In a smaller bowl, whisk together the egg, oil, vanilla extract, milk, and banana. Pour this mixture into the dry ingredients, add the apple and pecans, and stir well to combine.

4. Spoon the mixture evenly into the muffin holes and smooth over the top of each hole with a palette knife. Bake for 18–20 minutes or until light golden and a toothpick inserted into the center comes out clean. Leave in the pan for 5 minutes before turning out onto a wire rack to cool.

◄ **PER MUFFIN** ►
177 cal; 5 g fat (including 0.5 g saturated fat); 2 g fiber;
4 g protein; 30 g carbohydrates

CHERRY CHOCOLATE MUFFINS

*T*hese muffins remain fresh for a day. Freezing will keep them longer.

**MAKES 12 ■ PREPARATION TIME 20 minutes ■
COOKING TIME 15 minutes + cooling time**

---

canola oil spray
⅔ cup brown rice flour
½ cup gluten-free cornstarch
1½ teaspoons gluten-free baking powder
½ teaspoon baking soda
1 teaspoon xanthan gum
1½ tablespoons psyllium husks
⅓ cup superfine sugar
⅓ cup rice bran cereal
⅔ cup dried cherries
⅓ cup shredded coconut
¼ cup milk chocolate chips
1 egg, lightly beaten
½ cup low-fat milk
2½ tablespoons canola oil
1 teaspoon vanilla extract

1. Preheat the oven to 350°F. Coat a 12-hole (each ⅓-cup capacity) muffin pan with canola oil spray.
2. In a large mixing bowl, sift together the brown rice flour, cornstarch, baking powder, baking soda, and xanthan gum and stir to mix well. Sift a second time into another large bowl. Stir in the psyllium husks, sugar, rice bran cereal, cherries, coconut, and chocolate chips.
3. In a smaller bowl, whisk together the egg, milk, oil, and vanilla. Add the egg mixture to the dry ingredients and stir well to combine.
4. Spoon the mixture evenly into the muffin holes and smooth the top of each with a palette knife. Bake for 15 minutes or until golden and a toothpick inserted into the center comes out

clean. Leave in the pan for 5 minutes before turning out onto a wire rack to cool.

VARIATIONS

Omit the cherries and try:

- ⅔ cup fruit medley with the coconut and ¼ cup white chocolate chips instead of the milk chocolate chips
- ⅔ cup chopped dried apricots with the coconut and ¼ cup dark chocolate chips (omit milk chocolate chips)
- ⅔ cup chopped figs, ⅔ cup toasted flaked almonds (omit coconut), and ¼ cup dark chocolate chips (omit milk chocolate chips)

◄ **PER MUFFIN** ►
189 cal; 7 g fat (including 2.5 g saturated fat); 2 g fiber;
3 g protein; 30 g carbohydrates

CORN, CARROT, AND ONION MUFFINS

*T*hese muffins are quick to prepare and are a delicious snack. Enjoy them as a light lunch with a side serving of salad. They remain fresh for a day. Freezing will keep them longer.

MAKES 15 ■ **PREPARATION TIME 25 minutes** ■
COOKING TIME 25 minutes + cooling time

---

canola oil spray
⅔ cup rice flour
⅓ cup gluten-free cornstarch
⅓ cup soy flour
2 teaspoons gluten-free baking powder
1 teaspoon baking soda
1 teaspoon xanthan gum
2 teaspoons rice bran
2 teaspoons psyllium husks
1 cup polenta
3 tablespoons superfine sugar
11-ounce can corn kernels, drained
3 scallions, sliced
½ cup coarsely grated carrot (about 1 small carrot)
2½ tablespoons chopped parsley
¼ cup canola oil
1½ cups buttermilk
1 egg

1. Preheat the oven to 375°F. You will need two 12-hole (each ⅓-cup capacity) muffin pan trays. Coat 15 of the holes with canola oil spray.

2. In a large mixing bowl, sift together the rice flour, cornstarch, soy flour, baking powder, baking soda, xanthan gum, and rice bran. Stir to combine, then sift a second time into another large bowl. Mix in psyllium, polenta, and sugar. Add the vegetables and parsley, and stir well to combine.

3. In a smaller bowl, whisk together the oil, buttermilk, and egg. Pour into the dry ingredients and vegetables, and stir until just combined.

4. Spoon the mixture evenly into 15 muffin holes, smoothing the top of each with a palette knife. Bake for 20–25 minutes or until tops are slightly golden and a toothpick inserted into the center comes out clean. Leave in the pan for 5 minutes before turning out onto a wire rack to cool.

VARIATION

- You can substitute 1 cup fresh or frozen corn kernels for the canned corn.

◄ **PER MUFFIN** ►
163 cal; 5 g fat (including 1 g saturated fat); 1 g fiber;
5 g protein; 24 g carbohydrates

BANANA WALNUT LOAF

*F*ruit breads such as this make a satisfying after-school snack and are handy to toast for breakfast. Slice and serve warm or toasted topped with margarine or ricotta cheese. Light cream cheese or ricotta mixed with a little orange zest makes a delicious topping for this loaf.

MAKES 12 slices ■ **PREPARATION TIME 25 minutes** ■ **COOKING TIME 40 minutes + cooling time**

---

1 cup rice flour
½ cup gluten-free cornstarch
½ cup soy flour
2 teaspoons gluten-free baking powder
1 teaspoon baking soda
1 teaspoon xanthan gum
1½ teaspoons cinnamon
2 teaspoons psyllium husks
2 eggs
⅓ cup superfine sugar
¼ cup canola oil
¼ cup unsweetened cloudy apple juice
1 teaspoon vanilla extract
1 cup mashed banana (about 2–3 bananas, depending on size)
1 cup coarsely chopped walnuts

1. Preheat the oven to 375°F. Grease and line a 9-inch-by-5-inch-base loaf pan.

2. In a large mixing bowl, sift together the rice flour, cornstarch, soy flour, baking powder, baking soda, xanthan gum, and cinnamon into a large bowl. Stir to combine and then sift a second time into another large bowl. Stir in psyllium husks and make a well in the center.

3. In a smaller bowl, whisk together the eggs, sugar, oil, apple juice, and vanilla. Add the mashed banana and whisk again to combine well. Pour into the well in the dry ingredients and stir, using a wooden spoon, until combined. Stir in the walnuts.

4. Pour the mixture into the prepared pan, leveling the top with a palette knife. Bake for 40 minutes or until cooked and a toothpick inserted into the center comes out clean. Leave in the pan for 5 minutes before turning the loaf out onto a wire rack to cool.

◄ PER SLICE ►
253 cal; 14 g fat (including 1 g saturated fat); 1.5 g fiber;
7 g protein; 28 g carbohydrates

FRUIT LOAF

$\mathcal{W}$e are often asked what can be done to lower the GI of baked foods. This recipe is a good example—it replaces some of the flour with plenty of our favorite low-GI ingredients, including cloudy apple juice, dried fruit, and rice bran cereal. Cover the cake with foil if the top begins to darken during baking.

MAKES 12 slices ■ **PREPARATION TIME** 25 minutes ■
COOKING TIME 35 minutes + cooling time

½ cup unsweetened cloudy apple juice
¾ cup raisins
1 cup diced dried apricots
1 cup rice flour
⅓ cup gluten-free cornstarch
⅓ cup besan (chickpea) flour
2 teaspoons gluten-free baking powder
1 teaspoon baking soda
1 teaspoon xanthan gum
3 teaspoons apple pie spice
1½ tablespoons psyllium husks
½ cup firmly packed brown sugar
½ cup rice bran cereal, lightly crushed
2 eggs, lightly beaten
2½ tablespoons canola oil
½ cup reduced-fat milk
⅓ cup diced pitted prunes

1. Preheat the oven to 350°F. Grease and line the base of a 9-inch-by-5-inch-base loaf pan.
2. Heat the apple juice in a small saucepan and bring just to a boil. Add the raisins and apricots, remove from heat, stir, and set aside.
3. In a large mixing bowl, sift together the rice flour, cornstarch, besan flour, baking powder, baking soda, xanthan gum, and apple pie spice. Stir to combine and then sift a second time into another large bowl. Stir in the psyllium husks, sugar, and crushed bran cereal and mix well to combine. Make a well in the center.

4. In a smaller bowl, whisk together the eggs, oil, and milk. Pour into the dry ingredients, then add the dried fruit and apple juice mixture, and the prunes. Stir with a wooden spoon until well combined.

5. Pour the mixture into the prepared loaf pan and smooth the top with a palette knife. Bake for 25–30 minutes or until golden and a toothpick inserted into the center comes out clean. Leave in the pan for 5 minutes before turning out onto a wire rack to cool.

◄ PER SLICE ►
212 cal; 5 g fat (including 0.5 g saturated fat); 2.8 g fiber;
4 g protein; 38 g carbohydrates

Low-GI Gluten-free Baking Tips

- Sift the gluten-free flours twice as we suggest—it gives the dry ingredients a good airing.
- When baking, sift the dry ingredients first, and then most of the work is done!
- The ingredient list may seem long, but we use a mixture of gluten-free flours plus ingredients such as baking powder and xanthan gum to help with texture, as well as rice bran and psyllium husks to increase the fiber content.

BROWNIES

*T*here's nothing like a batch of brownies at the end of a long day. They make a wonderful after-school treat or a delicious dessert to nibble on with coffee or tea. As we say at the beginning of this chapter, treats are important—as long as they're just that, not an everyday food. As a finishing touch, place 2 teaspoons of gluten-free powdered sugar into a small, fine strainer and shake gently over each one.

MAKES 12 slices ■ **PREPARATION TIME** 20 minutes ■
COOKING TIME 25 minutes + cooling time

⅓ cup brown rice flour
⅓ cup potato flour
½ teaspoon gluten-free baking powder
¼ teaspoon baking soda
¼ teaspoon xanthan gum
¼ cup cocoa
⅔ cup almond meal
2 teaspoons psyllium husks
3½ ounces dark chocolate (63% cocoa), roughly chopped
8 tablespoons reduced-fat margarine
⅓ cup brown sugar
1 teaspoon vanilla extract
1 egg
½ cup buttermilk
pure powdered sugar or gluten-free powdered sugar mixture
(optional), to serve

1. Preheat the oven to 350°F. Grease and line an 8-inch-by-8-inch cake pan.

2. In a large mixing bowl, sift the brown rice flour, potato flour, baking powder, baking soda, xanthan gum, and cocoa. Stir to combine dry ingredients and sift a second time into another large bowl. Stir in the almond meal and psyllium husks, and set aside.

3. Melt the chocolate, margarine, and sugar in a medium to large saucepan on low heat, stirring until smooth. Remove from the heat and add the vanilla. Stir in the egg and then the dry ingredients mix. Pour in the buttermilk and combine well.

4. Spoon the brownie mixture into the prepared pan, smoothing the top evenly with a palette knife. Bake for 20 minutes or until the top is firm and a toothpick inserted into the center comes out clean. Leave in the pan to cool before dusting with powdered sugar, if you wish.

◄ PER BROWNIE WITHOUT POWDERED SUGAR ►
190 cal; 11 g fat (including 4 g saturated fat); 1.5 g fiber;
3 g protein; 18 g carbohydrates

MUESLI NUT COOKIES

*C*runchy cookies are very popular in lunchboxes. These are packed with nutrients and fiber and, as an after-school snack, will provide an energy boost before kids' sports training or homework. They will keep for a few days in an airtight container. If they become soft, you can "crisp" them up in a preheated 350°F oven for 4–5 minutes.

MAKES about 26 ■ **PREPARATION TIME** 20 minutes ■
COOKING TIME 25 minutes + cooling time

6½ tablespoons reduced-fat margarine
¼ cup honey
⅓ cup brown rice flour
⅓ cup gluten-free cornstarch
½ teaspoon gluten-free baking powder
½ teaspoon xanthan gum
1 teaspoon cinnamon
2½ tablespoons brown sugar
2 cups gluten-free low-GI muesli
2½ tablespoons almond meal
¼ cup chopped macadamia nuts
¼ cup chopped walnuts
1 egg, lightly beaten
½ teaspoon vanilla extract

1. Preheat the oven to 325°F. Line 2 baking trays with parchment paper.
2. Melt the margarine and honey in a small saucepan, stirring occasionally. Set aside to cool.
3. In a mixing bowl, sift the brown rice flour, cornstarch, baking powder, xanthan gum, and cinnamon. Stir to combine, then sift a second time into another bowl. Stir through the sugar, muesli, almond meal, macadamia nuts, and walnuts.
4. Pour the cooled margarine mix into the muesli mix, add the egg and the vanilla, and stir with a wooden spoon to combine.
5. Take 1 tablespoon of the mix, shape into a ball, flatten slightly, and place on a baking tray. Continue with remaining mix. Bake

for 18–20 minutes, swapping trays halfway during cooking, or until golden. Leave on trays for 10 minutes before transferring to a wire rack to cool.

◄ PER COOKIE ►
111 cal; 7 g fat (including 2 g saturated fat); 2 g fiber;
2 g protein; 10 g carbohydrates

APRICOT NUT SLICE

$\mathcal{D}$iane originally created this for our free online newsletter, GI News, and it was so popular with our readers there, we decided to include it in this book. The GI is probably moderate, because it uses sweet gluten-free cookies in the base.

MAKES 12 pieces ■ **PREPARATION TIME** 10 minutes ■ **COOKING TIME** 25 minutes

---

4½ ounces (about 8 medium) gluten-free sugar cookies, crushed into crumbs
⅓ cup brown rice flour
⅓ cup hazelnut meal
1 egg white
3 tablespoons reduced-fat margarine, melted

Filling

7 ounces dried apricots
2 ounces dried cherries
1 cup water
2 teaspoons superfine sugar
1 ounce flaked almonds

1. Preheat the oven to 350°F. Grease a 10-inch-by-5-inch-base loaf pan. Line the base and the two long sides with parchment paper and extend the paper about 1 inch above the edge of the pan to help with removing the slice when it is cooked and cooled.

2. To make the base: Combine the cookie crumbs, flour, and hazelnut meal in a medium bowl. Whisk the egg white until slightly foamy. Add the margarine and egg white to the crumbs and mix together, using your fingers to combine. Press the mixture into the base of the prepared pan. Bake for 10 minutes or until base is lightly browned.

3. For the topping: Place the apricots, cherries, and water in a small saucepan and bring to a boil. Simmer for 10 minutes until the fruit is soft, stirring occasionally to break up the fruit. Mix

in the sugar. Spread the filling evenly over the cooked base. Sprinkle the flaked almonds over the top.

4. Bake the slice for 15 minutes or until the almonds are lightly toasted. Leave in the pan to cool. Slice when cold and store in an airtight container.

◄ PER PIECE ►
177 cal; 8 g fat (including 1.5 g saturated fat); 2.5 g fiber;
3 g protein; 23 g carbohydrates

NO-BAKE CHOCOLATE CLUSTERS

*T*his is a recipe for making your own fruit chocolates. You will achieve the best results with a good-quality chocolate—one with 63% cocoa solids is ideal. A darker chocolate (around 70%) may be too bitter. You can buy amaranth breakfast cereal in health food stores and the health food aisle of supermarkets.

MAKES about 50 ■ **PREPARATION TIME** 10 minutes ■
COOKING TIME 5 minutes + setting time

---

14 ounces dark chocolate (63% cocoa)
½ cup raisins
½ cup dried cranberries
½ cup chopped dried apricots
½ cup chopped dried apples
¼ cup amaranth breakfast cereal (optional)

1. Melt the chocolate in a medium-sized bowl over a saucepan of simmering water, stirring occasionally, until the chocolate has melted and is smooth.
2. In a small bowl, combine the raisins, cranberries, apricots, apples, and amaranth (if using). Add to the melted chocolate and stir to combine and coat the fruit.
3. Place a heaping teaspoonful of the mix on a lined baking tray. Repeat with the remaining mixture, placing the clusters 1–1½ inches apart. Place in the refrigerator to set. Store the clusters in an airtight container in the refrigerator.

◄ PER CLUSTER WITHOUT AMARANTH ►
53 cal; 2.5 g fat (including 2 g saturated fat); 0.5 g fiber;
0.5 g protein; 7 g carbohydrates

Take 5

5 QUICK SNACKS

- Fresh fruit salad
- A handful of fresh or frozen grapes
- Celery, cucumber, or carrot sticks, or bell pepper wedges with hummus or a yogurt-based dip
- Smoothie (see our recipes, pages 84–86)
- Hummus on a gluten-free cracker

5 GRAB 'N' RUN SNACKS

- A piece of fruit, such as a juicy orange, small banana, large peach, or pear
- A handful of dried-fruit and nut mix
- A handful of dried apricots or apple rings, or raisins
- A tub of low-fat yogurt or a dairy dessert
- A small piece of low-fat cheese or string cheese

5 WARMING SNACKS

- An ear of corn
- A cup of gluten-free vegetable soup with a slice of gluten-free toast
- A toasted sandwich made with low-GI gluten-free bread
- A small can of baked beans or creamed corn
- A small serving of gluten-free noodles with vegetables

5 THIRST-QUENCHING SNACKS

- A small glass of fruit juice
- A glass of low-fat milk or calcium-enriched gluten-free soy milk
- A glass of ice water with a twist of lemon or lime
- A smoothie (see our recipes, pages 84–86)
- A caffe latte with low-fat milk

▪9▪

Light Meals and Lunches

*R*efueling at lunchtime helps you maintain those energy levels and concentration through the afternoon. It also reduces the temptation to snack mindlessly on an entire package of chips later in the day.

BEEF AND BEAN FAJITAS

This can be one of those "assemble your own" meals. Arrange the ingredients attractively on a big platter or in several small bowls and go for it.

MAKES 12 ■ PREPARATION TIME 25 minutes ■ COOKING TIME 15 minutes

---

1½ tablespoons olive oil
9 ounces lean rump steak, thinly sliced
1 red (Spanish) onion, sliced
1 red pepper, sliced
1 yellow pepper, sliced
1–2 jalapeno peppers (optional), seeded and finely chopped
¼ teaspoon chili powder
2 teaspoons sweet paprika
1 teaspoon ground cumin
1 teaspoon ground coriander
juice of 1 lime
2½ tablespoons tomato paste
½ teaspoon sugar
¼ cup chopped cilantro leaves
14-ounce can kidney beans, rinsed and drained
14-ounce can corn kernels, drained

To Serve
12 gluten-free white corn tortillas
1 quantity Easy Guacamole (see page 215)
½ cup grated low-fat tasty cheese
mixed salad leaves

1. Heat 2 teaspoons oil in a large frying pan. Add the meat and stir-fry for 3–4 minutes or until brown. Remove from the pan and set aside.

2. Add the remaining oil to the pan, add the onion, peppers, and jalapenos, if using, and cook for 3 minutes. Stir in the chili powder, paprika, cumin, ground coriander, lime juice, tomato paste, and sugar. Return all the meat to the pan and cook for 2–3 minutes. Stir in the cilantro leaves, kidney beans, and corn kernels, and stir until heated through.

3. Heat the tortillas following the package instructions (either in the microwave for 30 seconds or wrap in foil and warm in the oven for a few minutes).

4. On each tortilla, place some of the beef mixture on one side, add 1 tablespoon guacamole, a little cheese, and salad leaves, and roll up. Alternatively, arrange the tortillas on a large platter, and in several bowls the beef mixture, guacamole, salad leaves, and cheese, and let everyone make their own.

◄ PER FAJITA WITH GUACAMOLE ►
215 cal; 10 g fat (including 3 g saturated fat); 3.5 g fiber;
10 g protein; 20 g carbohydrates

CHICKEN TACOS

Tacos are another "make your own" favorite. Or you can assemble them beforehand and serve them ready-made on a large platter. We also include a variation for Chili Bean Tacos for vegetarians.

SERVES 4 ■ PREPARATION TIME 20 minutes ■ **COOKING TIME** 20 minutes

---

2 teaspoons olive oil
2 cloves garlic, crushed
9 ounces ground chicken
1½ teaspoons ground cumin
1 teaspoon oregano
¼ teaspoon ground chili (optional)
½ red pepper, diced
½ green pepper, diced
14-ounce can diced tomatoes
1½ tablespoons tomato paste
¼ teaspoon sugar
freshly ground black pepper
14-ounce can kidney beans, drained and rinsed

To Serve
12 gluten-free taco shells
1 quantity Easy Guacamole (page 125)
2 cups shredded iceberg lettuce
1 cup reduced-fat grated tasty cheese
2 tomatoes, diced

1. Heat the oil in a large frying pan, add garlic and chicken, and cook for 3–4 minutes, stirring and breaking up chicken. Add the cumin, oregano, and chili, and cook for 1 minute more. Add the peppers, canned tomatoes, tomato paste, sugar, and pepper, stir, bring to a boil, and simmer for 10 minutes. Stir in the kidney beans until heated through.

2. Meanwhile, line a tray with parchment paper, place the taco shells on the tray, and bake in the oven for 4–5 minutes or until warm (not hot) and crisp.

3. To serve, fill the shells with the chicken mixture. Top with gua-camole, lettuce, cheese, and diced tomatoes.

VARIATION
- To make Chili Bean Tacos, replace the chicken with an extra can of kidney beans or 14-ounce can drained lentils.

◄ **PER TACO WITH SERVING SUGGESTIONS** ►
192 cal; 10 g fat (including 2.5 g saturated fat); 3 g fiber;
10 g protein; 13 g carbohydrates

FALAFEL WRAPS

*M*ade with chickpeas, falafel are a low-GI favorite. And because they are equally tasty hot or cold, they are ideal for lunchboxes and after-school snacks on their own or in a wrap.

SERVES 4 (makes 12) ■ **PREPARATION TIME** 15 minutes ■
COOKING TIME 20 minutes

14-ounce can chickpeas, drained and rinsed
2 cloves garlic, chopped
1 teaspoon ground cumin
½ teaspoon ground coriander
2½ tablespoons finely chopped parsley
1½ tablespoons chopped cilantro leaves
½ teaspoon gluten-free baking powder
olive oil spray

To Serve
Hummus (see page 215)
4 large gluten-free wraps
Pistachio and Quinoa Tabbouleh (see page 150)

1. Preheat the oven to 400°F. Line a baking tray with parchment paper.
2. Place the chickpeas and garlic in a food processor and process until fairly smooth. Transfer to a bowl and combine well with the cumin, coriander, chopped parsley, chopped cilantro leaves, and baking powder.
3. To make the falafel patties, take 1 tablespoon of the mixture, roll into a ball, and flatten slightly. Place on the prepared tray. Continue with remaining mixture. Spray the falafel patties with olive oil spray. Bake for 20 minutes, turning the patties over halfway during cooking time. The patties should be slightly crisp on the outside and lightly golden. Transfer to a plate and set aside.
4. Spread 2 tablespoons of hummus over 1 side of each wrap. Top each with about ⅓ cup tabbouleh and 3 falafels. Roll up the wraps and serve.

VARIATIONS

- For extra oomph, add a tablespoon of a tangy gluten-free salsa or sauce.
- Serve with tahini rather than hummus.

◄ **PER FALAFEL PATTY** ►
29 cal; 1 g fat (including 0 g saturated fat); 1 g fiber;
1 g protein; 3 g carbohydrates

CORN AND CILANTRO FRITTERS

Our timing for this recipe is based on cooking the fritters one at a time. But if you have a very large frying pan, you could cook two at a time.

SERVES 4 (makes 8) ■ PREPARATION TIME 25 minutes ■ COOKING TIME 20 minutes

---

1 large ear of corn (to make 1 cup corn kernels)
½ red pepper, diced
¼ cup chopped cilantro
1 red chili, deseeded and finely diced
3 scallions, thinly sliced
½ cup buckwheat flour
1 teaspoon gluten-free baking powder
½ teaspoon paprika
3 eggs, lightly beaten
⅔ cup buttermilk
freshly ground black pepper
about 2½ tablespoons canola oil

To Serve
4 ounces low-fat plain yogurt
1½ tablespoons gluten-free sweet chili sauce
1½ tablespoons chopped cilantro
green salad with vinaigrette dressing

1. Cut the corn kernels off the cob. Combine the corn, pepper, cilantro, chili, and scallions in a large bowl, and set aside.

2. Sift the buckwheat flour, baking powder, and paprika into a medium bowl, and make a well in the center.

3. Whisk together the eggs and buttermilk in a smaller bowl, season with freshly ground black pepper, and pour into the dry ingredient mix. Whisk to combine well. Stir the combined mixture into the vegetables and mix well.

4. Heat 2 teaspoons oil in a nonstick frying pan. Pour in ¼ cup of the mixture and, using a palette knife, spread to around 5 inches in diameter. Cook on low to medium heat for 1 minute on each side or until light golden-brown. Remove and drain on a paper towel. Repeat with the remaining batter, adding 1–2 extra teaspoons of oil as needed to the pan.

5. Meanwhile, mix the yogurt with the sweet chili sauce.

6. Place 2 fritters on each plate and serve topped with some yogurt mix, a sprinkle of chopped cilantro, and a serving of salad.

VARIATION

- You can substitute an 11-ounce can of drained corn or 1 cup frozen corn kernels for the ear of corn.

◄ **PER SERVING WITHOUT SALAD** ►
309 cal; 15 g fat (including 2.5 g saturated fat); 2 g fiber;
13 g protein; 15 g carbohydrates

INDIVIDUAL SPANISH TORTILLAS

$\mathcal{T}$hese little tortillas are a meal in themselves. Canola oil spray works really well, preventing the tortillas from sticking or leaving a mess. Steam the potato and sweet potato rather than boiling, if you prefer.

**MAKES 8 ■ PREPARATION TIME 20 minutes ■
COOKING TIME 30 minutes + cooling time**

---

canola oil spray
5½ ounces small new potatoes, peeled and chopped into ½-inch chunks
7 ounces sweet potato, peeled and chopped into ½-inch chunks
2 teaspoons canola oil
1 small red pepper, diced
3 strips (2 ounces) lean shortcut bacon, all visible fat removed, diced
3 ounces spinach leaves
6 eggs
½ cup low-fat milk
freshly ground black pepper

1. Preheat the oven to 350°F. Spray 8 holes of a 12-hole muffin pan (each ¾-cup capacity) with canola oil spray.
2. Place the potatoes and sweet potatoes in a small saucepan of boiling water, and cook for about 8 minutes or until just tender. Drain.
3. In a large frying pan, heat the oil, add the pepper and bacon, and cook for 1 minute. Add the potatoes and sweet potatoes, and brown a little, about 2–3 minutes.
4. Remove from the heat, stir in the spinach, then pour the mixture into a large bowl.
5. Whisk the eggs and milk together in a small bowl, and season.
6. Spoon about 2–3 tablespoons of the vegetable mixture into each muffin pan hole. Pour the egg mixture over. Bake for 20 minutes or until just set. Leave in the pan for 5 minutes before turning out onto a wire rack to cool.

VARIATIONS
- Replace the sweet potato with butternut squash.
- To make a vegetarian version, omit the bacon. Cook 1 chopped onion for 3–4 minutes, and then add other vegetables.

◄ PER TORTILLA ►
113 cal; 5 g fat (including 1.5 g saturated fat); 1 g fiber;
8 g protein; 8 g carbohydrates

ITALIAN MEATBALLS IN TOMATO SAUCE

This classic family favorite is delicious served with rice and a big crispy green salad. The ground mixture also makes 8 meat patties (using ¼ cup of mixture for each). Grill or pan-fry to make the burgers. We used a pre-made Italian spice mix for this, but give the recipe in Basics (page 218) a try if you want to make your own.

SERVES 4 ■ PREPARATION TIME 10 minutes ■ COOKING TIME 20 minutes

18 ounces lean ground beef
⅓ cup fresh gluten-free low-GI breadcrumbs
¼ teaspoon chili powder
1 teaspoon Italian herbs or 1 teaspoon oregano
2 cloves garlic, crushed
¼ cup tomato paste

Tomato Sauce
2 cups tomato passata (or tomato purée)
1 cup gluten-free reduced-salt chicken stock
1 teaspoon sugar
freshly ground black pepper
2½ tablespoons chopped parsley

To Serve
1 cup low-GI rice, cooked
green salad with vinaigrette dressing

1. In a large bowl, combine the ground beef, breadcrumbs, chili powder, Italian herb mix, garlic, and tomato paste, and mix well. Roll heaping tablespoons of the mixture into balls. Chill.
2. Meanwhile, place the passata, stock, sugar, and some pepper into a medium saucepan and bring to a boil. Arrange the meatballs in the sauce, reduce the heat, and simmer, uncovered, for 15 minutes or until meatballs are cooked through. Stir in the parsley.
3. Serve with rice and salad.

◄ **PER SERVING WITH MEATBALLS, SAUCE, AND RICE** ►
314 cal; 11 g fat (including 5 g saturated fat); 2 g fiber;
29 g protein; 25 g carbohydrates

CHICKEN NUGGETS WITH SALAD

These tangy nuggets are great for lunch or a light meal. They are also perfect for parties or finger-food events. Diane's daughter, Ava, thinks that they are so delicious they should be served with a big sign reading for kids ONLY.

MAKES 16 ■ **PREPARATION TIME** 15 minutes ■ **COOKING TIME** 10 minutes

---

½ cup dried gluten-free breadcrumbs
2 tablespoons sesame seeds
14 ounces chicken breast, chopped roughly
1 tablespoon reduced-salt gluten-free tamari
1 tablespoon gluten-free plum sauce

To Serve
vegetable sticks
cherry tomatoes
gluten-free tomato sauce or gluten-free sweet chili sauce

1. Preheat the oven to 350°F. Line a baking tray with parchment paper.

2. Mix the breadcrumbs and sesame seeds together and place on a large flat dish.

3. Place the chicken, tamari, and plum sauce in a food processor and process until well mixed and the chicken is minced.

4. Wet your hands and take a tablespoon of the chicken mixture, form into a disc about the size of a matchbox and roll it in the breadcrumb mix. Place the nugget on a baking tray and continue with the remaining mix.

5. Bake nuggets for 10–12 minutes or until chicken is cooked through and the crumbs are golden and crunchy. Serve with sauce for dipping, along with vegetable sticks such as carrot, cucumber, celery, pepper, and cherry tomatoes.

◄ **PER NUGGET WITHOUT VEGETABLES** ►
53 cal; 2.5 g fat (including 0.5 g saturated fat); 0.5 g fiber;
6 g protein; 2 g carbohydrates

SALMON AND SQUASH PATTIES WITH LIMA BEAN SALAD

*T*o make the amount of mashed squash you need for this recipe, boil, steam, or microwave 3½ ounces peeled butternut squash. Drain off any excess liquid and mash with a fork.

MAKES 4 patties ■ PREPARATION TIME 25 minutes ■
CHILLING TIME 30 minutes ■ COOKING TIME 25 minutes

7-ounce can pink salmon, drained
14-ounce can lima beans, drained
⅓ cup mashed butternut squash
2 scallions, chopped
2 teaspoons rice bran
½ teaspoon gluten-free curry powder
1½ tablespoons brown rice flour
2 teaspoons canola oil
3 ounces wild arugula

Lima Bean Salad
2½ tablespoons balsamic vinegar
1½ tablespoon extra-virgin olive oil
1 small red pepper, chopped
½ small red onion, diced
1 small avocado, diced

1. In a medium bowl, mash the salmon and ½ cup lima beans with a fork. (Reserve the remaining beans for the salad.)
2. Mix in the squash, scallions, bran, and curry powder. Divide the mix into 4 portions and shape each into a patty about 3–3½ inches across. Chill in the refrigerator for 30 minutes.
3. Meanwhile, preheat the oven to 350°F. Line a baking tray with parchment paper. Dust the patties with brown rice flour. In a large frying pan, heat the canola oil, add the patties, and cook on medium heat for 1 minute each side or until just golden brown. Place the patties on a baking tray and cook in the oven for 20–25 minutes or until firm.

4. To make the Lima Bean Salad, whisk together the balsamic vinegar and oil. Combine the pepper, onion, avocado, and reserved lima beans in a small bowl. Toss with half of the balsamic dressing.

5. Place the arugula in a bowl and toss with the remaining dressing. Divide the arugula equally among four serving plates, and top each with a salmon patty and a large spoonful of lima bean salad.

◄ PER SERVING ►
313 cal; 24 g fat (including 5 g saturated fat); 3.5 g fiber;
15 g protein; 7 g carbohydrates

CHICKEN MANGO RICE PAPER ROLLS

MAKES 12 ■ PREPARATION TIME 30 minutes ■ COOKING TIME 10 minutes

1 (9-ounce) chicken breast
2 ounces bean thread noodles
1 mango, peeled and cut into short strips
2 ounces (about 6) snow peas, trimmed and sliced diagonally in half
¼ cup shredded mint
12 round 8-inch rice papers

Dipping Sauce
⅓ cup lime juice
1½ tablespoons fish sauce
1½ tablespoons superfine sugar

1. Put about 1½ cups water in a small saucepan (enough to cover the chicken) and bring to a boil. Add the chicken, reduce the heat, and simmer, covered, for 10 minutes. Set aside to cool in the pan. When chicken is cool enough to handle, shred and then refrigerate.

2. Place the noodles in a heatproof bowl and cover with boiling water. Leave for 3–4 minutes or until soft, then drain. Rinse the noodles under running water to cool, drain again, and cut into short lengths (½–1 inch).

3. To make the dipping sauce, combine all ingredients in a bowl and stir until sugar dissolves. Set aside.

4. Place all filling ingredients on a counter. Dip the wrappers one at a time in a shallow bowl of warm water for 10–15 seconds or until just soft. Drain off excess water and place on a clean surface.

5. Place about 1 tablespoon shredded chicken, 1 heaping tea-spoon noodles, 2 strips mango, 2 pieces snow pea, and 1 tea-spoon mint on the rice paper, about 1 inch in from the base of the wrapper. Fold up the bottom of the wrapper, then fold in the sides and roll up to enclose the filling. Place on a tray and cover

with paper towels. Continue with remaining filling and wrappers. Serve the rolls on a platter with the dipping sauce.

◄ **PER ROLL WITH DIPPING SAUCE** ►
75 cal; 1 g fat (including 0.5 g saturated fat); 0.5 g fiber;
6 g protein; 10 g carbohydrates

CARROT, AVOCADO, AND SNOW PEA RICE PAPER ROLLS

*S*queeze some lime juice over the avocado after it has been sliced to prevent it from turning brown.

MAKES 12 ■ PREPARATION TIME 30 minutes

---

2 ounces bean thread noodles
1 small carrot, cut into short, thin sticks
1 avocado, cut into short, thin slices
squeeze of lime juice for the avocado
½ bunch garlic chives, cut into 3
2 ounces (about 6) snow peas, sliced diagonally in half
2 ounces snow pea sprouts, ends trimmed
12 round 8-inch rice papers

Dipping Sauce
¼ cup gluten-free sweet chili sauce
¼ cup lime juice
2 teaspoons reduced-salt gluten-free tamari

1. Place bean thread noodles in a heatproof bowl and cover with boiling water. Leave for 3–4 minutes or until noodles are soft, then drain. Rinse under running water to cool, then drain and cut noodles into short lengths (½–1 in).
2. To make the dipping sauce, combine all ingredients in a bowl and set aside.
3. Place all the filling ingredients on a counter. Half-fill a large bowl with warm water. Dip one wrapper in the water for 10–15 seconds or until it is just soft. Drain off excess water and place on a clean surface.
4. Place a heaping teaspoon of noodles, and a few pieces each of the carrot, avocado, garlic chives, snow peas, and sprouts on the wrapper, about 1 inch in from the base of the wrapper. Fold up the bottom of the wrapper, then fold in the sides and roll up to

enclose filling. Place on a tray and cover with paper towels. Continue with remaining filling and wrappers.

5. Serve the rolls on a platter with the dipping sauce.

◄ PER ROLL WITH DIPPING SAUCE ►
86 cal; 5 g fat (including 1 g saturated fat); 1 g fiber;
2 g protein; 8 g carbohydrates

TANGY TUNA RICE PAPER ROLLS

MAKES 12 ■ PREPARATION TIME 30 minutes

2 ounces bean thread noodles
7-ounce can tuna in brine or spring water, drained
½ cup grated carrot (about 1 small carrot)
½ cup shredded Chinese cabbage
2 scallions, thinly sliced
1½ tablespoons chopped mint
¼ cup lemon juice
2 teaspoons sesame oil
1 tablespoon honey
12 round 8-inch rice papers

Dipping Sauce
⅓ cup tomato sauce
1 tablespoon reduced-salt gluten-free tamari

1. Place bean thread noodles in a heatproof bowl and cover with boiling water. Leave for 3–4 minutes or until noodles are soft, then drain. Rinse under running water to cool, drain, and then cut noodles into small lengths.
2. In a large bowl, combine tuna, carrot, cabbage, scallions, and mint, and mix well.
3. In a small bowl, whisk together the juice, oil, and honey. Pour over the tuna mixture and stir through.
4. To make the dipping sauce, combine the ingredients in a bowl. Set aside.
5. Half-fill a large bowl with warm water. Dip one wrapper in the water for 10–15 seconds or until just soft. Drain off excess water and place on a clean surface.
6. Place ¼ cup of the tuna mixture on the wrapper, about 1 inch in from the base. Fold up the bottom of the wrapper, then fold in the sides and roll up to enclose the filling. Place on a tray and cover with paper towels. Continue with remaining filling and wrappers.

7. Serve the rolls on a platter with the dipping sauce.

◀ **PER ROLL WITH DIPPING SAUCE** ▶
70 cal; 1 g fat (including 0.5 g saturated fat); 0.5 g fiber;
5 g protein; 9 g carbohydrates

SUSHI WITH THREE FILLINGS

$\mathcal{L}$ow-GI rice is nearly as good as using sushi rice except it won't be quite as sticky. To make a dipping sauce to serve, mix a little reduced-salt tamari and wasabi together, to taste. The marinade from the tofu is also nice as a dipping sauce.

PREPARATION TIME 15 minutes ■ **COOKING TIME** 20 minutes
+ 10 minutes standing time

---

3 cups cooked low-GI rice, warm
¼ cup rice wine vinegar
1½ tablespoons superfine sugar
6 sheets toasted nori

Avocado and Tofu Filling (makes 4 rolls)

3½ ounces firm tofu, cut into 2 slices, then cut again in half lengthwise
2½ tablespoons reduced-salt gluten-free tamari
2½ tablespoons rice wine vinegar
1 clove garlic, crushed
½ avocado, thinly sliced
1 Lebanese cucumber, cut into short strips

Salmon Filling (makes 2 rolls)

2 ounces smoked salmon, sliced
½ avocado, thinly sliced

Tuna Filling (makes 2 rolls)

3½-ounce can (or nearest size) tuna in brine or spring water, drained
1½ tablespoons gluten-free low-fat mayonnaise or plain yogurt
1 dab of wasabi paste, or to taste
½ Lebanese cucumber, deseeded, cut into long strips

1. To marinate the tofu for the avocado and tofu filling, place the tofu in a small dish. Combine the tamari, rice wine vinegar, and garlic in a separate small dish, pour over the tofu, and place in the refrigerator to marinate for about 30 minutes. The longer you can leave it, the better.

2. Place the rice in a medium saucepan and cook following the package instructions, then let stand for 10 minutes.

3. Gently heat rice wine vinegar and sugar, stirring, until sugar dissolves. Gently fold the vinegar mixture into the rice. Spread rice over a tray, cover with plastic wrap, and leave to cool.

4. Run a bamboo sushi mat under water, shake off the excess water, and place on a flat surface. Place one nori sheet, rough side up and with a long end closest to you, on the mat. Using wet hands, place a quarter of the rice on the sheet, and pat down to cover the sheet, leaving 1½ inches at the top of the sheet. Press the rice firmly down on the sheet and make a slight indentation in the rice 1½ inches in from the bottom of the sheet closest to you.

5. **To make the avocado and tofu–filled rolls,** drain the tofu from the marinade. Place two pieces of tofu in the indentation, then a few slices of avocado and strips of cucumber. Roll up the sushi. Repeat to make the other rolls.

6. **To make the salmon-filled rolls,** place half the smoked salmon and half the avocado in the indentation along the rice. Using the bamboo mat, firmly roll up the sushi. Remove the mat. Using a wet knife, cut the roll into thick, equal slices. Repeat to make a second roll.

7. **To make the tuna-filled rolls,** combine the tuna with the mayonnaise and wasabi. Place half the cucumber strips and half the tuna in the indentation along the rice and roll up the sushi. Repeat to make the second roll.

◄ PER ROLL (CUT INTO 4 PIECES SUSHI) ►
Avocado and Tofu:
306 cal; 9 g fat (including 2 g saturated fat); 2 g fiber; 8 g protein; 47 g carbohydrates
Salmon:
306 cal; 9 g fat (including 2 g saturated fat); 2 g fiber; 8 g protein; 47 g carbohydrates
Tuna:
285 cal; 3 g fat (including 1 g saturated fat); 1 g fiber; 15 g protein; 48 g carbohydrates

Lunchbox Tips

ALTHOUGH GLUTEN-FREE breads are improving in texture, there's a general consensus that they aren't ideal for sandwiches, unless toasted. So when packing a lunch, try these ideas:

- Mini vegetable frittatas (include vegetables such as corn, sweet potato, a few chickpeas, green peas, zucchini, and bell pepper)
- Vegetable muffins
- Tuna or salmon and rice slice (mix together low-GI rice, tuna or salmon, peas, sweet corn, and egg, top with grated cheese, bake in oven, and cut into squares)
- Squash and salmon patties
- Homemade pasta salad with gluten-free pasta and plenty of veggies
- Homemade potato salad with small new potatoes, corn kernels, peas, and pepper strips
- Lentil and vegetable soup, or chicken and corn soup
- Baked beans with corn thins
- Vietnamese rice paper rolls
- California or sushi rolls
- Corn tortilla wrap spread with avocado and filled with pinto beans, shredded lettuce, diced cucumber, and grated cheese
- Gluten-free wrap filled with falafel, hummus, and Quinoa and Pistachio Tabbouleh (page 150)
- For a quick rice salad, use instant brown or basmati rice tossed in a vinaigrette dressing with corn kernels, red pepper strips, and scallions.

Add a piece of fruit or two, and a snack for midday break, and the lunchbox is ready to go.

·10·

Salads and Soups

_F_or a relaxing, informal meal in a bowl, you can't beat a soup or salad for healthy satisfaction.

THAI BEEF SALAD
WITH CHILI LIME DRESSING

This is a tangy light meal, and the leftovers are ideal for lunch or as a snack. It's an easy recipe to modify to suit your taste. Add more vegetables if you like, or rice vermicelli for a more substantial salad. Leftover salad can be stored in an airtight container in the refrigerator for up to 1 day.

SERVES 4 ■ PREPARATION TIME 20 minutes ■ COOKING TIME 10 minutes + resting time

---

canola oil spray
4 small (about 3½ ounces each) lean beef steaks
2 ounces dried rice vermicelli
1 medium carrot, peeled and cut into thin strips
1 medium Lebanese cucumber, cut into thin strips
1 medium red pepper, cut into thin strips
1 cup bean sprouts
1 bunch mint, leaves picked and roughly chopped
1 bunch cilantro, leaves picked and roughly chopped

Chili Lime Dressing
2½ tablespoons lime juice
2½ tablespoons fish sauce
1½ tablespoons grated palm sugar or raw sugar
2 teaspoons white wine vinegar
1 small fresh red chili, very finely chopped

1. Preheat a grill or heavy-based frying pan on medium-high and lightly coat with canola oil spray. Cook the steaks for 3–4 minutes on each side (depending on thickness) or to your liking.

2. Wrap in foil and set aside for 10 minutes to rest before slicing finely, cutting diagonally across the grain.

3. Meanwhile, prepare the rice vermicelli according to package instructions. Drain well and cut into short lengths.

4. To make the Chili Lime Dressing, whisk all ingredients together in a small bowl. The dressing should have a slightly sour taste with just a touch of sweetness and a little heat. If you like it tangier, add extra fish sauce, lime juice, or sugar to taste.

5. In a large serving bowl, combine the beef, rice vermicelli, carrot, cucumber, pepper, bean sprouts, mint, and cilantro. Toss well with the Chili Lime Dressing and serve.

VARIATION

■ For a vegetarian meal, replace the beef with an equivalent amount of marinated tofu.

◄ PER SERVING ►
236 cal; 8 g fat (including 2.5 g saturated fat); 2.5 g fiber;
24 g protein; 16 g carbohydrates

WARM POTATO SALAD WITH HERBS AND TOASTED HAZELNUTS

*T*he Dijon Dressing in this recipe is a favorite of our tester, Diane Temple. Using two vinegars does make a difference. Store leftover salad in an airtight container in the refrigerator for up to 1 day.

SERVES 4 ■ **PREPARATION TIME** 15 minutes ■ **COOKING TIME** 10–15 minutes

---

about 18 ounces small new potatoes, scrubbed and cut into thick slices
14-ounce can red kidney beans, drained and rinsed
1 avocado, peeled and sliced
2 scallions, finely sliced
2½ tablespoons roughly chopped flat-leaf (Italian) parsley
2½ tablespoons lightly toasted chopped hazelnuts

Dijon Dressing
2½ tablespoons olive oil
1½ tablespoons white wine vinegar
1½ tablespoon cider vinegar
1 teaspoon Dijon mustard
½ teaspoon (or to taste) superfine sugar
1 small clove garlic, crushed (optional)
pinch salt (optional)
freshly ground black pepper

1. Steam the potatoes, covered, for 10 minutes or until tender. Drain well.
2. Meanwhile, to make the Dijon Dressing, whisk all ingredients together in a small bowl.
3. Place the warm potato slices in a large serving bowl, add the beans, pour over the dressing, and stir through the potatoes so they are well coated with the dressing. Add the avocado slices, onions, and parsley, toss gently to combine, top with the toasted hazelnuts, and serve.

VARIATION

■ Replace the red kidney beans with lima beans; the avocado with 2 medium beets, roasted and diced; and the parsley with dill.

◄ **PER SERVING** ►
388 cal; 26 g fat (including 4.5 g saturated fat); 8 g fiber;
9 g protein; 26 g carbohydrates

CHICKEN PASTA SALAD
WITH MANGO SALSA

*M*ost (but not all) gluten-free pastas are made from corn or rice flour and have a high GI, which is why we like to combine them with ingredients we know will help reduce the overall GI.

SERVES 4 ■ **PREPARATION TIME** 20 minutes ■ **COOKING TIME** 20 minutes

---

1 (9-ounce) skinless chicken breast
1½ tablespoons olive oil
1–2 teaspoons Madras Curry Blend (see page 218)
5½ ounces gluten-free pasta shells, or your favorite shape
1 Lebanese cucumber, deseeded and diced into ½-inch pieces
1 mango, flesh diced
3½ ounces cherry tomatoes, halved
3½ ounces trimmed sugar snap peas, blanched
1 small red chili, deseeded and finely sliced (optional)
2–3 stems fresh mint leaves, torn
freshly ground black pepper

Dressing
2½ tablespoons lemon (or lime) juice
2½ tablespoons olive oil

1. Preheat the oven to 350°F.
2. Brush both sides of the chicken with oil and sprinkle with curry powder. Place the chicken in an ovenproof dish and bake for 20 minutes or until cooked. Let rest for 5–10 minutes, then slice.
3. Meanwhile, cook the pasta in a large saucepan of boiling water until al dente, following the package instructions for timing. Check a minute or two before the end of the cooking time. Drain in a colander and chill under running cold water to stop the cooking process. Drain well.
4. To make the dressing, combine the lemon or lime juice and oil in a small bowl and whisk together.

5. In a serving bowl, combine the cucumber, mango, tomatoes, peas, chili, pasta, chicken, and mint leaves. Pour over the dressing, add freshly ground black pepper to taste, and toss to combine.

◄ PER SERVING ►
383 cal; 18 g fat (includes saturated fat 3 g); 4 g fiber;
18 g protein; 38 g carbohydrates

CHICKEN AND RICE LETTUCE CUPS

*T*his is a great recipe for when you have leftover chicken. Prepare it in stages: You can cook the rice and the chicken the day before and store in airtight containers in the refrigerator. Store leftover salad in an airtight container in the refrigerator for up to 1 day.

SERVES 8 ■ PREPARATION TIME 15 minutes ■ COOKING TIME 40 minutes + 20–30 minutes cooling time

---

½ cup wild rice, rinsed and drained

1 cup brown rice, rinsed and drained

2 cups frozen corn and pea mix, thawed

1 (about 7 ounces) cooked skinless chicken breast fillet, shredded

1 green pepper, diced

1 red pepper, diced

1 Lebanese cucumber, deseeded and diced

6 scallions, finely chopped

¼ cup finely chopped fresh parsley

16 cup- or scoop-shaped iceberg lettuce leaves, washed, then chilled to crisp

Zesty Dressing

⅓ cup orange juice

¼ cup lemon juice

¼ cup olive oil

2 teaspoons finely grated ginger, or to taste

2 teaspoons lemon zest

2 teaspoons soft brown sugar, or to taste

salt and freshly ground black pepper

1. Cook the brown rice and wild rice in two separate saucepans, following the package instructions. Fluff with a fork and set aside to cool.

2. Steam the corn and peas for 1–2 minutes or until just al dente. Rinse immediately under cold running water to cool and stop the cooking process. Drain thoroughly.

3. To make the Zesty Dressing, whisk all ingredients together in a small bowl and season to taste.

4. In a serving bowl, combine the shredded chicken with the wild rice, brown rice, corn, peas, pepper, cucumber, scallion, and parsley. Pour over the dressing and toss well. Spoon the mixture into the lettuce cups and serve.

VARIATIONS
- Replace the chicken with flaked canned tuna or salmon, or with smoked trout.
- For a vegetarian meal, serve without the chicken.

◄ PER SERVING—2 LETTUCE CUPS ►
275 cal; 10 g fat (including 1.5 g saturated fat); 4 g fiber;
11 g protein; 34 g carbohydrates

Cooking Brown Rice and Wild Rice Together

IF THE BROWN rice and wild rice you buy require the same cooking time, you can cook them together using the absorption method. In a heavy-based saucepan, bring ⅓ cup wild rice and ⅔ cup brown rice to a boil in 2 cups water. Reduce the heat to very low, cover, and simmer for 40 minutes. Remove from the heat and let stand, covered, for another 20–30 minutes. Fluff with a fork.

PISTACHIO AND QUINOA TABBOULEH

Quinoa is a tiny, fast-cooking grain ideal in gluten-free dishes. It's not just low GI—it's also rich in nutrients, including protein. Enjoy this tabbouleh on its own, in iceberg lettuce-leaf scoops, in gluten-free wraps or pita pockets with hummus, or as a salad accompaniment to a barbecue. Store leftover salad in an airtight container in the refrigerator for up to 1 day.

**SERVES 6 ■ PREPARATION TIME 10 minutes ■
COOKING TIME 15 minutes + resting time**

---

1 cup quinoa, rinsed
juice of 1 lemon, or to taste
2½ tablespoons extra-virgin olive oil
freshly ground black pepper
½ cup roughly chopped pistachio nuts
1 cup chopped flat-leaf (Italian) parsley
½ cup chopped mint leaves, or to taste
1 small red (Spanish) onion, finely diced
2 large vine-ripened tomatoes, deseeded and chopped
1 medium Lebanese cucumber, deseeded and diced

To Serve
gluten-free wraps
hummus (see Basics, page 215)

1. Place the quinoa in a medium saucepan and cover with 2 cups of water. Bring to a boil, then reduce the heat and simmer for 10–15 minutes or until the grains are just tender and translucent and all the water is absorbed. Remove from the heat and let rest, covered, for 5–10 minutes. Fluff with a fork.
2. Meanwhile, whisk together the lemon juice and oil and season to taste.
3. Transfer the warm quinoa to a serving bowl with the nuts, parsley, mint, onion, tomato, cucumber, and dressing. Mix well to combine. Serve in a bowl, or with gluten-free wraps and hummus, to scoop and wrap your salad if you like.

VARIATION

- For an even more colorful salad, use red quinoa (you'll find it in health food stores) and follow the cooking times suggested on the package.

◄ **PER SERVING OF TABBOULEH ONLY** ►
275 cal; 14 g fat (including 1.5 g saturated fat); 5.5 g fiber;
8 g protein; 25 g carbohydrates

TUNA PASTA NIÇOISE

*B*eans and vinaigrette-style dressing help to lower the GI of this gluten-free pasta recipe. Store leftover salad in an airtight container in the refrigerator for up to 1 day.

SERVES 4 ■ PREPARATION TIME 15 minutes ■ COOKING TIME 10 minutes

---

7 ounces gluten-free pasta shapes
¼ cup vinaigrette dressing
6-ounce can Italian-style tuna in oil, drained and flaked
14-ounce can cannellini beans, drained and rinsed
1 small fennel bulb, finely sliced
1 small red (Spanish) onion, very finely sliced
¼ cup pitted kalamata olives
2 stems basil, leaves picked and roughly chopped
2 anchovy fillets, roughly chopped (optional)
1½ tablespoons capers, rinsed
2 hard-boiled eggs, quartered
12 green beans, steamed 3 minutes

1. Cook the pasta in a large saucepan of boiling water, following the package instructions and testing 1–2 minutes before end of cooking, until al dente. Drain in a colander.
2. Place in a large serving bowl. While pasta is still warm, toss with half the vinaigrette dressing.
3. Add the tuna, cannellini beans, fennel, onion, olives, basil, anchovies (if using), and capers, and toss to combine well. Top with the eggs and green beans, and sprinkle over the remaining dressing.

VARIATIONS
■ Replace the tuna with the same amount of canned salmon or smoked trout.
■ Replace the beans with chickpeas.
■ For a vegetarian option, omit the tuna and anchovies and add 2 or 3 extra hard-boiled eggs.

◄ **PER SERVING** ►
408 cal; 10 g fat (including 2 g saturated fat); 4.5 g fiber;
24 g protein; 53 g carbohydrates

Pasta Salads

Pasta teams well with:

- Tomatoes, lima beans, arugula, and goat cheese tossed in a balsamic dressing
- Gluten-free ham, asparagus, and baby corn tossed in a vinaigrette dressing
- Tuna, snow peas, cherry tomatoes. and red kidney beans with tzatziki dressing
- Apple, celery, dried fruit, and walnuts in a yogurt dressing
- Sun-dried tomatoes, roasted red pepper strips, cannellini beans, spinach, onion, and basil in a red wine vinegar dressing
- Roasted pumpkin, pine nuts, chickpeas, and arugula in a balsamic dressing
- Chicken, orange slices, avocado, celery, and almonds in a zesty citrus dressing

LENTIL AND FETA SALAD

We like to use lentils that hold their shape well when cooked for salads. Good choices are French green lentils or Puy lentils. If using brown lentils, watch the cooking time—you don't want them to get too soft for a salad. Store leftover salad in an airtight container in the refrigerator for up to 1 day.

**SERVES 4 ■ PREPARATION TIME 15 minutes ■
COOKING TIME 25 minutes + cooling time**

---

1 cup French green or Puy lentils
1 red pepper, diced
1 green pepper, diced
1 green chili, deseeded and finely chopped (optional)
1 small red (Spanish) onion, finely sliced
12 cherry tomatoes, quartered
¼ cup finely chopped cilantro
⅓ cup feta, crumbled

Balsamic Dressing
2½ tablespoons olive oil
1½ tablespoons balsamic vinegar
1½ tablespoons lemon juice
freshly ground black pepper

1. In a medium saucepan, bring the lentils to a boil with 2 cups water, stirring occasionally. Reduce the heat, cover, and simmer for about 20 minutes or until tender but firm to the bite. Remove from the heat, drain well, and set aside to cool.
2. Meanwhile, to make the dressing, whisk all ingredients together in a small bowl.
3. In a large serving bowl, combine the lentils, peppers, chili (if using), onion, cherry tomatoes, and cilantro. Pour over the dressing and toss well to combine. Top with crumbled feta and serve.

◄ PER SERVING ►
288 cal; 14 g fat (including 4 g saturated fat); 8.5 g fiber;
16 g protein; 22 g carbohydrates

Salad Days

DID YOU KNOW there's more to salad than leafy greens?

- Starting a meal with a mixed garden salad before moving on to the main course helps to fill you up, and you will eat less overall.

- Eating a side salad with your meal—especially if it's a high-GI meal—will help to keep your blood glucose levels under control. This is because the salad dressing acids, such as the lemon juice or vinegar, slow down stomach emptying, thereby slowing the digestion of starch in the meal you are eating.

VELVETY SQUASH SOUP

*T*his soup is one of Kate's favorites — and her clients love it too, if requests for recipe sheets are anything to go by! Purée the soup for about 10 seconds to achieve that creamy, velvety texture. Top each serving with a dollop of low-fat plain yogurt, if you like, then sprinkle with cilantro. If you make the soup the day before, store in the refrigerator in an airtight container, then reheat and serve.

SERVES 6 ■ PREPARATION TIME 15 minutes **■ COOKING TIME** 45 minutes

2½ tablespoons olive oil
2 medium onions chopped
1-inch piece ginger, peeled and grated
1 tablespoon curry powder
18 ounces butternut squash, peeled and diced
18 ounces sweet potato, peeled and diced
2 stalks celery, sliced
1 cup split red lentils, picked over and rinsed
3 cups gluten-free reduced-salt chicken or vegetable stock
freshly ground black pepper
2½ tablespoons finely chopped fresh cilantro (or parsley), to serve

1. Heat the olive oil in a large saucepan over medium heat. Add the onion, ginger, and curry powder, reduce the heat, and gently cook for 6–8 minutes or until onion is soft and golden. (Be careful it doesn't burn.)

2. Add the squash, sweet potato, celery, and red lentils to the pan, stir well to combine, and cook another minute. Pour in the stock and 3 cups water, and bring to a boil. Reduce heat to low and simmer gently for 30 minutes or until the vegetables are soft. Season to taste.

3. When cool, purée the soup in batches in a food processor or blender, then reheat gently. Spoon the soup into bowls, sprinkle with chopped cilantro, and serve.

◄ **PER SERVING** ►
253 cal; 7 g fat (includes 1 g saturated fat); 7.5 g fiber;
12 g protein; 32 g carbohydrates

ITALIAN RICE AND LENTIL SOUP

*T*his is one of those soups your spoon almost stands up in. If that's too thick for you, just add more water. The secret of success is to make sure the onions really are soft before you proceed any further with the cooking. If you make the soup the day before, store in the refrigerator in an airtight container, then simply reheat and serve. Passata, tomato purée, is an Italian cooking sauce. You'll find it in all good supermarkets.

SERVES 6 ■ PREPARATION TIME 5–10 minutes ■
COOKING TIME 30 minutes

1½ tablespoons olive oil
2 onions, finely chopped
1 clove garlic, finely chopped
1½ ounces lean pancetta or bacon, visible fat removed, finely
    chopped
1 cup passata
¼ cup finely chopped parsley
2 cups gluten-free reduced-salt beef stock
½ cup carnaroli or arborio rice
2 (14-ounce) cans lentils, drained and rinsed
freshly ground black pepper
¼ cup grated Parmesan cheese, to serve

1. Heat the olive oil in a large saucepan on medium heat. Add the onion and garlic, reduce the heat, and cook for 10–12 minutes or until golden and soft. Add the pancetta and cook 1 minute more. Add the passata and parsley and cook another minute, stirring occasionally with a wooden spoon.
2. Add the stock and 3 cups water and bring to a boil. Reduce the heat, add the rice, and simmer for 8–10 minutes. Add the lentils and cook 5 more minutes or until the rice is cooked al dente and the lentils are heated through. Season to taste.
3. Spoon into bowls, sprinkle with Parmesan cheese, and serve.

VARIATION

- For a vegetarian version, omit the pancetta and use a reduced-salt vegetable stock instead of the beef stock.

◄ **PER SERVING** ►
250 cal; 6 g fat (including 1.5 g saturated fat); 3.5 g fiber;
9 g protein; 39 g carbohydrates

SHRIMP LAKSA

$\mathcal{L}$aksas are popular spicy soups that originated in Malaysia and Singapore, and now seem to be available everywhere. The thick white noodles seem to be preferred in restaurants, but we like making laksa with the thin ones and adding more vegetables. They are slightly more manageable to eat, too!

SERVES 4 ■ **PREPARATION TIME** 15 minutes ■ **COOKING TIME** 10 minutes

---

4½ ounces dried rice-stick noodles
⅓ cup gluten-free red curry paste
11 ounces peeled and deveined shrimp
2½ cups gluten-free reduced-salt chicken stock
1⅛ cups light coconut milk
1 large carrot, cut into short thin sticks
3½ ounces shiitake mushrooms, thinly sliced
4½ ounces green beans, diagonally sliced
3 baby bok choy, leaves separated, washed, shredded
1 teaspoon brown sugar (optional)
1¼ cups bean sprouts
½ cup picked cilantro leaves, roughly chopped
lime wedges

1. Cook the noodles in a large saucepan of boiling water for 2 minutes or until just tender. Drain well. Divide the noodles among 4 large serving bowls.

2. Heat a large wok over high heat. Add the curry paste and shrimp, and stir-fry for 3 minutes or until the shrimp change color. Add the stock and coconut milk, and bring to a simmer. Add the carrot, mushrooms, and beans and cook for 2 minutes. Add the bok choy and cook for 1 more minute or until just wilted. Remove from the heat and stir in the sugar, if using.

3. Divide the vegetables and shrimp among the bowls. Ladle the broth into each bowl. Top with the bean sprouts and cilantro, and serve with the lime wedges.

VARIATIONS
- Replace the shrimp with 11 ounces skinless chicken breast, cut into thin strips.
- For a vegetarian version, replace the shrimp with 11 ounces tofu and the chicken stock with reduced-salt vegetable stock.

◄ PER SERVING ►
359 cal; 10 g fat (including 1.5 g saturated fat); 6.5 g fiber;
27 g protein; 37 g carbohydrates

MEXICAN BLACK BEAN SOUP
WITH CORN

*B*lack beans, also called turtle beans, have a mild earthy flavor when cooked and are widely used throughout Latin America and the Caribbean. Soaking overnight shortens the cooking time. If you make the soup the day before, store in the refrigerator in an airtight container, then simply reheat and serve the next day.

SERVES 6 ■ Soaking time overnight ■ **PREPARATION TIME** 15 minutes ■ **COOKING TIME** 1 hour 15 minutes

---

1 cup dried black beans, soaked overnight
2½ tablespoons olive oil
2 red (Spanish) onions, chopped
2 cloves garlic, crushed
2 teaspoons ground oregano
2 teaspoons ground cumin
1 red chili, deseeded and finely sliced, or to taste
1 red pepper, diced
1 green pepper, diced
2 stalks celery, sliced
2 dried bay leaves
3 cups gluten-free reduced-salt vegetable stock
1 cup corn kernels
2 squares of chocolate (70% cocoa) or 2 teaspoons unsweetened cocoa powder
½ cup orange juice
¼ cup finely chopped cilantro (or parsley)

1. Drain the black beans from the soaking water, then rinse under cold water and drain again.

2. Heat the oil in a large, heavy-based saucepan over medium heat. Add the onion and garlic, reduce the heat, and cook for 8–10 minutes or until the onion is soft and translucent. Add the oregano, cumin, and chili and cook 1 more minute or until aromatic. Add the peppers, celery, black beans, bay leaves, stock, and 2 cups water and bring to a boil. Reduce the heat and simmer, uncovered, for 50 minutes. Stir in the corn kernels and continue cooking for 10 minutes or until the beans are tender.

3. Remove the bay leaves from the soup. Stir in the chocolate, orange juice, and cilantro and simmer for 1–2 minutes. Ladle into bowls and serve.

VARIATION

■ If you want to use canned black beans, here's how. Add the canned beans and corn kernels in Step 2 with the peppers, celery, bay leaves, stock and 2 cups water. Bring to a boil, then reduce the heat and simmer, uncovered, for 15 minutes. Stir in the chocolate, orange juice, and cilantro, and simmer for 1–2 more minutes before serving.

◄ **PER SERVING** ►
231 cal; 7 g fat (including 1 g saturated fat); 10.5 g fiber;
9 g protein; 32 g carbohydrates

For That Authentic Mexican Flavor

YOU REALLY NEED chipotle chilies (smoked jalapenos) canned in a thick adobo sauce for an authentic Mexican flavor. To make your own, see the recipe in Basics (page 217). You can find chipotle chilies in your grocery store in the Mexican food section.

CHUNKY TOMATO SOUP
WITH CHICKPEAS

*M*oroccan spice blends are usually a combination of paprika, pepper, cassia (cinnamon), cumin, cloves, coriander, cardamom, and nutmeg. You can add them to soups, meat and seafood dishes, or rice. Or use them to coat meat, before browning, for a casserole. This is quite a hearty soup, so add extra water or stock if you wish. If you make the soup the day before, store in the refrigerator in an airtight container, then simply heat through and serve the next day.

SERVES 8 ■ **PREPARATION TIME** 10 minutes ■ **COOKING TIME** 40 minutes

2½ tablespoons olive oil
2 red (Spanish) onions, chopped
2 cloves garlic, crushed
1-inch piece ginger, peeled and grated
1 medium (9 ounces) sweet potato, peeled and diced
2 celery stalks, sliced
2 medium carrots, scrubbed and diced
28-ounce can peeled Roma tomatoes, drained, chopped, and juice reserved
2 teaspoons pure floral honey
2 teaspoons Moroccan spice blend
3 cups gluten-free reduced-salt vegetable stock
14-ounce can chickpeas, rinsed and drained
¼ cup roughly chopped cilantro
freshly ground black pepper

To Serve
creamy style low-fat plain yogurt (allow 1 tablespoon per person)
1 tablespoon finely chopped cilantro

1. Heat the oil in a large, heavy-based saucepan over medium heat. Add the onion, garlic, and ginger, reduce the heat, and cook for 8–10 minutes or until the onion is soft and translucent. Add the sweet potato, celery and carrots, and cook for 1–2 more minutes, stirring occasionally.

2. Stir in the tomatoes, honey, and spice mix. Pour in the stock and 3 cups water. Bring to a boil, then reduce the heat and simmer gently for 10–15 minutes or until the vegetables are cooked. Add the chickpeas and cilantro, and cook 5 more minutes. Season to taste and serve in bowls with a dollop of creamy yogurt and a sprinkle of cilantro.

VARIATIONS

■ For a creamy tomato soup, set soup aside to cool, then blend in batches in a food processor or blender. Reheat in the saucepan and serve.

■ For a stronger tomato flavor, add 1 tablespoon tomato paste at Step 2.

◄ **PER SERVING** ►
149 cal; 5 g fat (including 1 g saturated fat); 4.5 g fiber;
5 g protein; 17 g carbohydrates

Souped Up

WHEN YOU ARE making soup, it actually doesn't require any extra time to make a larger amount. Leftovers are ideal for lunch the next day. Or freeze the extra soup for easy meals when there's no time to cook and you need a meal in a hurry. Tasty, low-GI soups to try (as well as our recipes here) include:

■ Lentil and spinach
■ Split pea and ham
■ Asian-style long or won ton soup with tofu and noodles
■ Bean soup
■ Tomato soup
■ Minestrone (with gluten-free pasta)

Freeze in individual portions in labeled airtight containers for up to 2 months. Thaw in the refrigerator before reheating.

EASY CHICKEN AND CORN SOUP

This is a quick and easy, hearty soup you can make with a takeout chicken if you are short on time. Make sure that you buy a gluten-free chicken (without any stuffing or seasoning with gluten). Add extra water for a more liquid soup.

SERVES 6 ■ PREPARATION TIME 10 minutes ■ COOKING TIME 10 minutes

---

7 ounces thick, dried rice-stick noodles

4 cups gluten-free reduced-salt chicken stock

2 (about 14 ounces) cooked skinless chicken breast fillets, shredded or finely sliced on the diagonal

1½ tablespoons gluten-free soy sauce

2 cups fresh or frozen corn kernels

2 ounces snow pea sprouts

2 scallions, finely sliced

1. Cook the noodles following package instructions. Drain and divide among 4 large serving bowls.

2. Meanwhile, in a large saucepan, bring the stock with 1 cup water to a boil. Reduce the heat and add the chicken, soy sauce, and corn kernels. Simmer for 4 minutes or until the chicken is heated through and the corn is cooked. Stir in the snow pea sprouts and cook 1 more minute. Ladle the soup evenly into the bowls, over the rice noodles, top with scallion slices and serve immediately.

◄ **PER SERVING** ►
272 cal; 5 g fat (including 1 g saturated fat); 2.5 g fiber;
19 g protein; 36 g carbohydrates

•11•

Main Dishes

*W*hat's for dinner? Try these main meals that are filled with flavor and bursting with nutrients along with a healthy balance of carbs, protein, and the right fats.

PUTTING IT ON THE PLATE

A basic main meal eaten by most of us—whether it's traditional Western fare, or one with Mediterranean or Asian flavors—consists of some sort of meat with vegetables, and potato, rice, or pasta. There's nothing wrong with this as a starting point, but fine-tuning the proportions a little to match the plate model below will ensure a healthy, balanced meal.

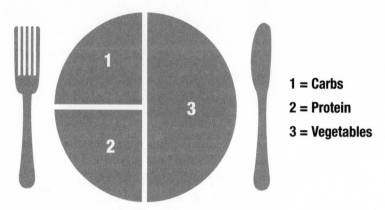

1 = Carbs
2 = Protein
3 = Vegetables

What is the plate model? We didn't create it, but we use and recommend it because it's simple and it works. It's an easy-to-learn aid to visualizing what to put on your plate. It is adaptable to different cuisines and is useful when eating out.

You can use it for any serving sizes, so long as you keep the food to the proportions shown. In addition, choose foods in line with the key recommendations, such as opting for good fats, cutting back on saturated fat, and being choosy about your carbs, and you will be right on track to eating a healthy diet and managing your weight.

1. **Carbohydrate-rich foods**—bread, cereals, and other starchy foods, such as potatoes, legumes, sweet corn, pasta, rice, and noodles—choose low-GI types
2. **Protein-rich foods**—meat, chicken, fish, eggs, tofu, and alternatives, such as legumes, milk, or yogurt
3. **Vegetables**

Quick and Easy Quinoa

QUINOA (PRONOUNCED KEEN-WAH) is a small, round, quick-cooking grain somewhat similar in color to sesame seeds. It's a nutritional powerhouse—an excellent source of low-GI carbs (GI 51), fiber, and protein, and rich in B vitamins and minerals including iron, phosphorus, magnesium, and zinc. You can buy quinoa flakes and quinoa flour, but these products haven't been GI tested yet. Health and organic food stores and larger supermarkets are the best places to shop for quinoa. You may find it's a little more expensive than other grains. It cooks in about 10–15 minutes (follow the package instructions) and has a light, chewy texture and slightly nutty flavor.

- Substitute quinoa for rice or other grains for gluten-free soups, stuffed vegetables, salads, stews, and even in a "rice" pudding or porridge.
- To serve as a side dish for four, rinse 1 cup of quinoa. Drain, place the grains in a medium pot with 2 cups of water, and bring to a boil. Reduce heat, cover, and leave to barely simmer until all the water has been absorbed.
- For a richer flavor, toast quinoa (but don't let it burn) in a dry pan for a minute or two before cooking as above.

CRANBERRY CHICKEN WITH QUINOA

$\mathcal{W}$e have allowed for 1 small chicken breast per person. But eat to appetite and if you have leftovers, this dish is delicious the next day—hot or cold.

SERVES 4 ■ PREPARATION TIME 30 minutes ■ **COOKING TIME** 30 minutes

---

¼ cup (about ½ small) coarsely grated Granny Smith apple
¼ cup dried cranberries
2½ tablespoons finely chopped walnuts
1 finely chopped scallion
1½ tablespoons finely chopped parsley
4 small (7 ounces each) skinless, boneless chicken breasts
1 red (Spanish) onion, sliced into thin wedges
a little olive oil
freshly ground black pepper
½ cup gluten-free, reduced-salt chicken stock
⅓ cup white wine

Quinoa Pilaf
2 teaspoons olive oil
1 small red (Spanish) onion, chopped
1 cup quinoa, washed and drained
2 teaspoons chopped sage
2 cups gluten-free reduced-salt chicken stock
1½ tablespoons chopped parsley

To Serve
steamed green beans and carrots

1. Preheat the oven to 400°F.
2. Combine apple, cranberries, walnuts, scallion, and parsley in a bowl.
3. Cut a deep slit (not all the way through) along the length of each chicken breast and spread with the apple filling. Use toothpicks to secure the openings.
4. Place the chicken in an ovenproof baking dish and surround with the onion wedges. Brush the chicken with olive oil and

grind some pepper over it. Combine the stock and wine in a small bowl and pour over the chicken. Bake for 25–30 minutes or until chicken is cooked through.

5. Meanwhile, to make the quinoa pilaf, heat the oil in a medium saucepan and add the onion. Cook for 3–4 minutes or until soft and golden (don't let the onion burn). Add the quinoa and sage, stir, add the stock, and bring to a boil. Reduce the heat, cover, and simmer for 12–15 minutes. Let stand for 5 minutes and then fluff the quinoa with a fork. Stir through the parsley.

6. Remove toothpicks from the chicken and slice each breast diagonally into 2 pieces.

7. To serve, spoon about ½ cup quinoa pilaf onto each plate, top with 1–2 slices of chicken, and drizzle with a little of the cooking sauce. Serve with beans and carrots.

◀ **PER SERVING WITH BEANS AND CARROTS** ▶
629 cal; 22 g fat (including 4.5 g saturated fat); 8.7 g fiber;
52 g protein; 48 g carbohydrates

GRILLED LEMON CHICKEN SKEWERS

*W*e've allowed an hour to marinate the chicken, but if you have the time, leave it a little longer to absorb the flavors of the marinade. The skewer enters the meat 3–4 times, like a needle threading through cloth.

SERVES 4 ■ PREPARATION TIME 25 minutes ■ MARINATING TIME 1 hour
■ COOKING TIME 30 minutes + standing time

---

21 ounces skinless, boneless chicken breasts (2 large)

Marinade
1 teaspoon finely grated lemon rind
½ cup lemon juice
1 teaspoon chopped fresh rosemary
1 tablespoon Dijon mustard
2 cloves garlic, crushed
1½ tablespoons olive oil

Bean and Asparagus Pilaf
1 bunch asparagus, cut into 1-inch pieces
4 ounces (about 12) green beans, trimmed and cut into 1-inch
pieces
2 teaspoons olive oil
1 onion, chopped
1 clove garlic, crushed
1 cup basmati rice
2 cups gluten-free, reduced-salt chicken stock
2½ tablespoons chopped parsley

To Serve
green salad with vinaigrette dressing

1. Soak 12 wooden skewers in water for 30 minutes.
2. Meanwhile, slice each chicken breast into 6-by-½-inch-thick long slices. You should have 12 long slices. Place 4 pieces on a sheet of plastic wrap, and cover with another sheet of plastic wrap. Use a rolling pin or mallet to flatten the pieces to about ¼-inch thick. Repeat with the remaining slices.

3. To make the marinade, combine all the ingredients in a medium bowl. Reserve ¼ cup of the mixture and set aside.

4. Add the chicken to remaining marinade in the bowl and chill in the refrigerator for 1 hour.

5. Meanwhile, to make the pilaf, steam the asparagus and beans for 2–3 minutes or until tender. Drain, rinse under cold water, and set aside.

6. Heat the oil in a medium saucepan. Add the onion and cook for 3–4 minutes or until soft and golden. Add the garlic and rice, and cook for 1 more minute, stirring. Add the stock, bring to a boil, then reduce the heat to low and simmer, covered, for 15 minutes. Let stand for 5 minutes. Stir through the beans, asparagus, parsley, and reserved marinade. Set aside, keeping warm.

7. Thread the chicken onto the skewers. Heat the grill and cook chicken each side for 2 minutes or until golden and cooked through.

8. To serve, spoon about ½ cup pilaf onto each plate, top with chicken, and serve with the salad.

◄ PER SERVING WITHOUT SALAD ►
485 cal; 16 g fat (including 3.5 g saturated fat); 2.5 g fiber;
38 g protein; 46 g carbohydrates

HERB FISH PACKETS WITH FENNEL, BEAN, AND TOMATO SALAD

*P*ackets not only make fish easy to cook, but they are fun to unwrap at the table, too. The parcels should cook in 15 minutes in a preheated oven, but times can vary a little depending on the thickness of the fish. The fish is cooked when it flakes easily with a fork.

SERVES 4 ■ PREPARATION TIME 25 minutes ■ COOKING TIME 15 minutes

¼ cup finely chopped parsley
1½ tablespoons chopped fennel leaves
2 teaspoons lemon rind
¼ teaspoon chili flakes
1 clove garlic, crushed
1½ tablespoons extra-virgin olive oil
freshly ground black pepper
4 (5-ounce) whitefish fillets

Fennel, Bean, and Tomato Salad
1 fennel bulb, thinly sliced
1 pint cherry tomatoes, quartered
14-ounce can (or nearest size) four-bean mix, rinsed and drained
1½ tablespoons baby capers
1 teaspoon lemon rind
¼ cup lemon juice
1½ tablespoons extra-virgin olive oil

To Serve
8 small new potatoes (optional)

1. Preheat the oven to 400°F. Tear 4 squares of parchment paper (about 12 inches by 12 inches).
2. In a small bowl, combine the parsley, fennel leaves, lemon rind, chili, garlic, and oil, and season to taste with freshly ground black pepper.
3. Place a piece of fish on each square of baking paper and spread the herb mix evenly over each. Fold and wrap the baking paper

securely to enclose the fish. Arrange the packets on a baking tray and bake for 15 minutes.

4. To make the salad, combine the fennel, tomatoes, beans, capers, and lemon rind in a serving bowl. Whisk together the lemon juice and oil in a small bowl, and toss through salad.

5. Place a fish packet on each plate with a generous scoop or two of salad alongside and a couple of steamed potatoes for extra carbs, if you wish.

◄ PER SERVING WITHOUT POTATO ►
326 cal; 13 g fat (including 2.5 g saturated fat); 7 g fiber;
36 g protein; 13 g carbohydrates

EASY TUNA BAKE

$\mathcal{E}$very family seems to have its own version of a comforting tuna bake—the perfect meal on a wintry evening when everyone is a bit tired after a long day. Make it with low-GI gluten-free pasta if you can. If it's not available, don't worry; we have added lots of other low-GI ingredients, such as milk, corn, and peas, to reduce the GI of this tasty dish.

SERVES 4 ■ PREPARATION TIME 25 minutes ■ COOKING TIME 55 minutes

---

olive oil spray
1 cup (3 ounces) gluten-free pasta spirals (or small shapes like macaroni)
2 7-ounce cans tuna in oil, drained, flaked
1 small red pepper, diced
3 scallions, sliced
⅓ cup gluten-free cornstarch
2 cups reduced-fat milk
⅓ cup finely grated Parmesan cheese
¼ cup finely chopped parsley
freshly ground black pepper
2 cups frozen corn and pea mix
1 tablespoon Dijon mustard

Topping
⅔ cup fresh gluten-free low-GI breadcrumbs
½ teaspoon paprika
1 tablespoon reduced-fat margarine

1. Preheat the oven to 350°F. Spray a 9-cup-capacity baking dish with olive oil spray.

2. Cook the pasta according to the directions on the package until only just al dente (remember you are going to be baking it as well), drain, cover, and set aside.

3. In a large bowl combine the tuna, peppers, and scallions.

4. Stir the cornstarch with a little of the milk in a small bowl until it dissolves. Heat the remaining milk in a large saucepan and bring just to a boil. Add the cornstarch mixture and stir until it boils, then reduce the heat to low and simmer for 1 minute while continuing to stir. Turn off the heat and stir in the cheese, parsley, and freshly ground black pepper.

5. Add the tuna mixture to the saucepan along with the corn and pea mix, mustard, and the pasta and combine well. Spoon the mixture into the prepared baking dish and smooth the top.

6. For the topping, combine breadcrumbs and paprika and rub in margarine. Sprinkle this evenly over the tuna mixture. Bake in the oven for 40 minutes or until the top is golden and crunchy. Serve with a garden salad

VARIATIONS

- Replace the frozen pea and corn mix with 11-ounce can corn, drained, and 1 cup frozen peas.
- To make the tuna bake more child-friendly for little ones, substitute the breadcrumb topping with a mix of crushed gluten-free snack chips, such as chickpea chips and a sprinkle of reduced-fat cheddar cheese.

◄ PER SERVING ►
565 cal; 22 g fat (including 5.5 g saturated fat); 6.5 g fiber;
40 g protein; 49 g carbohydrates

FRUITY LAMB CASSEROLE

*W*hen you are making a casserole, after the meat is browned, the pan is usually "deglazed." This means you add liquid such as wine or stock to loosen and dissolve the brown bits on the base formed during cooking. This way you enjoy all the flavor. You can find premade chermoula spice blends at Middle Eastern specialty stores.

SERVES 4 ■ **PREPARATION TIME** 20 minutes ■ **COOKING TIME** 1½ hours

---

1½ tablespoons olive oil
18 ounces trimmed diced lamb shoulder
1 onion, chopped
¼ cup red wine
2 cloves garlic, crushed
2½ tablespoons chermoula spice mix
2 cups gluten-free reduced-salt chicken stock
7 ounces sweet potato, peeled and chopped into 1-inch chunks
1 large parsnip, peeled and chopped into ½-inch chunks
2 small zucchinis, sliced into 1-inch chunks
3 ounces dried apricots
3 ounces pitted prunes
1½ ounces currants
2½ tablespoons chopped parsley

Mint Yogurt
6-ounce tub low-fat plain yogurt
1½ tablespoons finely chopped mint
1 teaspoon finely grated lemon zest
freshly ground black pepper

To Serve
steamed baby broccoli (Broccolini)

1. Heat the oil in a large saucepan. Add half the lamb pieces, and brown on all sides for about 3 minutes. Spoon into a dish and set aside. Repeat with the remaining lamb and keep warm.
2. To deglaze the pan, add the onion and wine and let it cook for 3–4 minutes on low heat. Add the garlic and chermoula spice mix and cook for 1 minute more, stirring regularly.

3. Return the meat to the pan with the stock, stir to combine, and bring to a boil. Reduce the heat to low, cover, and simmer gently for 50 minutes. Add the sweet potato, parsnip, zucchinis, dried apricots, pitted prunes, and currants, and bring back to a boil. Reduce the heat to low, cover, and simmer for 20 minutes more. Remove the lid and cook, uncovered, for 5 minutes. Stir in parsley.

4. To make the Mint Yogurt, combine the yogurt, mint, and lemon zest in a small serving bowl and season to taste.

5. Serve the casserole topped with a dollop of Mint Yogurt and lots of steamed baby broccoli or your favorite green vegetable alongside.

◄ **PER SERVING WITH YOGURT AND BABY BROCCOLI** ►
458 cal; 12 g fat (including 4 g saturated fat); 10.5 g fiber;
36 g protein; 42 g carbohydrates

GREEK-STYLE BEEF SKEWERS

*A*llow 4 pieces of meat, 5 pieces of pepper, and 2 pieces of mushroom per skewer.

SERVES 4 ■ PREPARATION TIME 30 minutes ■ MARINATING TIME 30 minutes ■ COOKING TIME 10 minutes

---

14 ounces lean beef rump, cut into 1-inch cubes
1 small red pepper, cut into 1-inch pieces
1 small green pepper, cut into 1-inch pieces
8 button mushrooms, cut in half

Herb Rub
1½ tablespoons dried oregano
2 teaspoons dried mint
1 tablespoon lemon zest
3 cloves garlic, crushed
2 tablespoons olive oil
2½ tablespoons lemon juice

Tomato and Bean Salad
3 small tomatoes, quartered
2 Lebanese cucumbers, sliced
1 small red (Spanish) onion, halved and thinly sliced
14-ounce can lima beans, drained and rinsed
¼ cup pitted kalamata olives
2½ tablespoons extra-virgin olive oil
2½ tablespoons lemon juice
1½ tablespoons white wine vinegar
½ teaspoon dried oregano

To Serve
8 steamed small new potatoes or gluten-free wraps

1. Place 8 long wooden skewers in water and set aside to soak for 30 minutes.
2. Meanwhile, to make the Herb Rub, combine the dried oregano, dried mint, lemon zest, garlic, olive oil, and lemon juice in a medium bowl. Add the beef, and mix well so that all the meat

is thoroughly coated. Cover and marinate in the refrigerator for 30 minutes, or longer if time permits.

3. To make the Tomato and Bean Salad, combine the tomatoes, cucumber, onion, beans, and olives in a serving bowl. Whisk together the oil, lemon juice, vinegar, and oregano in a small bowl. Pour over the salad and toss well.

4. Thread each skewer with beef cubes, peppers, and mushrooms, alternating each ingredient and starting with pepper.

5. Heat a grill on medium-high heat and brush with a little oil. Cook the kebabs, turning frequently, for 8 minutes or until meat is done to your liking. Serve immediately with salad and with 1–2 wraps or potatoes per person, if you wish.

◄ **PER SERVING WITH GLUTEN-FREE WRAPS** ►
494 cal; 24 g fat (including 5 g saturated fat); 5.5 g fiber;
28 g protein; 38 g carbohydrates

LAMB CURRY
WITH SPINACH RICE PILAF

We used mild curry powder in this recipe. If you can't find it, you can make your own blend. It is worth the effort for the flavor and aroma, without the heat. See Basics (page 218).

SERVES 4 ■ PREPARATION TIME 25 minutes ■ **COOKING TIME** 35 minutes

---

2 tablespoons gluten-free curry powder
14 ounces lamb fillet, diced into 1-inch pieces
1½ tablespoons canola oil
1 onion, chopped
2 cloves garlic, crushed
1 teaspoon grated ginger
2 carrots, chopped into 1-inch chunks
14-ounce can chopped tomatoes
2 cups cauliflower florets
¾ cup gluten-free reduced-salt chicken stock
1 cup frozen green peas

Spinach Rice Pilaf
1½ tablespoons canola oil
1 onion, chopped
½ cup basmati rice
1 cup gluten-free reduced-salt chicken stock
1 bay leaf
14-ounce can lentils, drained and rinsed
2 ounces (about 2 cups) baby spinach leaves

1. Sprinkle 2 teaspoons of the curry powder over the lamb to coat the pieces lightly. Heat 2 teaspoons of the oil in a large, heavy-based saucepan, add the lamb, and brown both sides for 2–3 minutes in 2 batches. Spoon the browned meat into a dish, cover, and set aside, keeping warm.

2. Heat the remaining oil in the pan. Add the onion and cook for 3–4 minutes until soft and golden. Add the garlic, ginger, remaining curry powder, and carrots, and cook, stirring, for 1 minute.

3. Return the meat to the pan with the tomatoes, cauliflower, and stock. Bring to a boil, then reduce the heat to low, cover, and simmer gently for 20 minutes. Add the peas and cook for another 2 minutes.

4. Meanwhile, to make the rice pilaf, heat the oil in a medium saucepan. Add the onion and cook for 3–4 minutes until soft and golden. Add the rice and cook, stirring, for another 1 minute. Add the stock and bay leaf and bring to a boil. Reduce the heat to low, cover, and simmer very gently for 15 minutes.

5. Stir in the lentils, heat through, and then stir in the spinach.

6. To serve, spoon a little pilaf on each plate and top with the curry.

VARIATION
- To make Curried Spinach Rice Pilaf, add 1 teaspoon curry powder to the pan when adding the rice.

◄ **PER SERVING** ►
451 cal; 17 g fat (including 4 g saturated fat); 9 g fiber;
31 g protein; 38 g carbohydrates

PORK WITH GLAZED APPLE AND CANNELLINI MASH

*C*loudy apple juice is a wonderful ingredient in savory dishes and baking, because it adds a touch of sweetness. We now know that cloudy apple juice has almost four times more antioxidants than clear apple juice because it retains its healthy pulp, with all the fiber.

**SERVES 4 ■ PREPARATION TIME 15 minutes ■
MARINATING TIME 30 minutes ■ COOKING TIME 25 minutes**

½ cup unsweetened cloudy apple juice
1½ tablespoons gluten-free reduced-salt tamari
1½ tablespoons maple syrup
½ teaspoon ground fennel
freshly ground black pepper
2 (10-ounce) pork fillets
1½ tablespoons olive oil
3 Granny Smith apples, quartered, cored, and sliced into thick wedges
1–2 tablespoons gluten-free, reduced-salt chicken stock

Cannellini Mash
2 cups frozen fava beans
14-ounce can cannellini beans, drained and rinsed
1 teaspoon reduced-fat margarine
¼ teaspoon ground fennel, optional

To Serve
steamed green beans
scrubbed and steamed baby carrots

1. Preheat the oven to 400°F. Line an ovenproof baking tray with parchment paper.
2. In a small bowl, combine the apple juice, tamari, maple syrup, and fennel, and season with pepper; reserve half. Place the pork fillets in a dish long enough to fit them, brush well with the other half of the marinade, cover, and marinate in the refrigerator for 30 minutes, or longer if time permits.

3. To make the Cannellini Mash, bring a saucepan of water to a boil, add the fava beans, and cook for 3 minutes. Drain and refresh under cold running water. When cool enough to handle, peel the skin from the beans. Combine the fava beans with the cannellini beans in a medium bowl and mash with a fork (it should have some texture). Set aside.

4. In a large frying pan, heat 2 teaspoons of oil, add the pork fillets and cook for 3–4 minutes, turning to make sure they are browned all over. Transfer to the baking tray and roast for 15 minutes. Cover with foil and set aside to rest.

5. Meanwhile, heat the remaining oil in the same frying pan. Add the apples and cook, stirring occasionally, for 12 minutes or until just tender. If the apples begin to stick, add 1–2 tablespoons of chicken stock. When the apples are cooked, add the reserved marinade. Let it bubble for a few seconds until it turns syrupy and then remove pan from heat and set aside.

6. To heat the Cannellini Mash, melt the margarine in a small saucepan. Add the mash and ground fennel, if using, and stir until heated through.

7. To serve, spoon a little mash on each plate, slice the pork on the diagonal, top with the apple, and drizzle over the syrupy juices. Serve with beans and carrots or your favorite vegetables.

◄ PER SERVING WITH BEANS AND CARROTS ►
436 cal; 10 g fat (including 2 g saturated fat); 9 g fiber;
45 g protein; 38 g carbohydrates

MOROCCAN SEAFOOD STEW

*W*e used a gluten-free seafood mix from a seafood store (rather than a frozen mix).

SERVES 4 ■ PREPARATION TIME 20 minutes ■ COOKING TIME 20 minutes

---

2 teaspoons olive oil
1 onion, chopped
1 fennel bulb, sliced
1 carrot, diced
2 cloves garlic, crushed
2 long red chilies, deseeded and finely chopped
2 teaspoons ground cumin
2 teaspoons ground coriander
¼ teaspoon cinnamon
1 cup water or gluten-free reduced-salt fish stock
18 ounces gluten-free seafood mix
2 tomatoes, diced
4 ounces sugar snap peas, cut in half
14-ounce can chickpeas, drained and rinsed
1 ounce (about 1½ cups) arugula
1 ounce (about 1 cup) spinach
2½ tablespoons chopped cilantro
lemon wedges

1. Heat the oil in a large, heavy-based saucepan. Add the onion and cook for 2–3 minutes. Add the fennel, carrot, garlic, chili, and spices, and cook for 1 minute more. Gradually add the stock, stirring, and then bring to a boil. Reduce the heat to low and simmer for 10 minutes, stirring occasionally.
2. Add the seafood mix and tomatoes, and cook for 3 minutes or until seafood has just cooked. In the last minute, add sugar snap peas. Then stir in chickpeas, arugula, and spinach until heated through. Stir in the cilantro.
3. Ladle the stew into bowls and serve with lemon wedges alongside.

◄ PER SERVING ►
307 cal; 8 g fat (including 1.5 g saturated fat); 8 g fiber;
38 g protein; 18 g carbohydrates

Oodles of Noodles

GLUTEN-FREE NOODLES (rice, buckwheat, or bean thread) are a great standby for quick meals. Served with fish, chicken, tofu, or lean meat and plenty of vegetables, a soup, salad, or stir-fry based on noodles gives you a healthy balance of smart carbs, fats, and proteins plus some fiber and essential vitamins and minerals. To cook, follow the instructions on the package, because times vary depending on types and thickness. Some noodles only need swirling under running warm water to separate, or soaking in hot (but not boiling) water to soften before you serve them or add to stir-fries. Others need to be boiled. Like pasta, they are usually best just tender, almost al dente, so keep an eye on the clock.

It's all too easy to slurp, gulp, twirl, and overeat noodles, so keep those portion sizes moderate. Although they are a low- to moderate-GI choice themselves, eating a huge amount will have a marked effect on your blood glucose. Instead of piling your plate with noodles, serve plenty of vegetables—a cup of noodles combined with lots of mixed vegetables can turn into three cups of a noodle-based meal and fit into any adult's or teenager's daily diet. Remember when planning meals that the sauces you serve with noodles and how you cook them (if they are crisp they are deep-fried) can provide a lot more calories than the noodles themselves.

PORK, BOK CHOY, AND NOODLE STIR-FRY

*T*his stir-fry really is a one-pot wonder. Not only do you use one frying pan or wok, but at the end you have a nourishing and satisfying meal with lots of vegetables—all in one bowl. Older children can help with the slicing.

SERVES 4 ■ PREPARATION TIME 20 minutes ■ COOKING TIME 15 minutes

---

7 ounces dry rice noodles

2½ tablespoons gluten-free reduced-salt tamari

2½ tablespoons gluten-free sweet chili sauce

1 teaspoon sesame oil

1½ tablespoons canola oil

18 ounces pork fillet, sliced thinly

1 red (Spanish) onion, sliced into thin wedges

2 teaspoons finely grated fresh ginger

1 red pepper, sliced into thin strips

4 ounces (or use nearest sized container) baby corn, sliced in half lengthwise

5 ounces snow peas, trimmed, sliced diagonally in half

1 bunch baby bok choy, trimmed, halved at stem joint, stem bases removed, leaves and stems sliced

⅓ cup toasted cashews, chopped roughly

1. Prepare the noodles according to package directions, drain, and set aside.
2. In a small bowl, combine the tamari, sweet chili sauce, and sesame oil and set aside.
3. In a large frying pan or wok, heat 2 teaspoons of canola oil. Add half the pork strips and stir-fry for 1–2 minutes or until just cooked. Spoon into a heatproof bowl and set aside. Repeat with the remaining pork.
4. Heat the remaining oil in the pan over medium-high heat. Add the onion and stir-fry for 2 minutes. Add the ginger, pepper, and corn, and stir-fry for about 1 minute. Add the snow peas and bok choy stems, and stir-fry for 1 more minute. (Add a little water or gluten-free reduced-salt chicken stock to pan if it starts to stick.)

5. Return the pork to the pan with tamari mix, bok choy leaves, and the noodles. Toss until well combined and heated through.

6. Spoon into serving bowls and serve sprinkled with cashews.

VARIATION
- To make a vegetarian version, Tofu, Bok Choy, and Noodle Stir-fry, replace the pork with 10 ounces firm tofu, drained and cut into 1-inch cubes.

◄ **PER SERVING** ►
474 cal; 15 g fat (including 2.5 g saturated fat); 5 g fiber;
36 g protein; 45 g carbohydrates

SQUASH, RICOTTA, AND LENTIL LASAGNA

A lasagna can seem like a lot of effort when you are pressed for time. But it's such a favorite on wintry evenings and a great (and economical) way to feed a hungry crowd. To save time, you can make the lentil sauce and bake the squash the night before so all you need to do the next day is assemble the dish and pop it in the oven.

SERVES 6–8 ■ PREPARATION TIME 35 minutes ■ COOKING TIME 1¾ hours

---

olive oil spray
14 ounces peeled butternut squash, sliced thinly
1½ tablespoons olive oil
2 teaspoons chopped fresh rosemary
freshly ground black pepper
1 large onion, chopped
1 carrot, halved lengthwise, then thinly sliced
2 cloves garlic, crushed
2½ tablespoons tomato paste
14-ounce can chopped tomatoes
14-ounce can lentils, drained and rinsed
½ teaspoon sugar
3 ounces (about 3 cups) baby spinach leaves
¼ cup chopped fresh parsley
2 cups low-fat ricotta cheese
1 egg
½ cup skim milk
½ cup finely grated Parmesan cheese
8-ounce package gluten-free lasagna noodles

To Serve
green, mixed leaf salad with a vinaigrette dressing

1. Preheat the oven to 400°F. Line a baking tray with baking paper. Grease an 8-inch-by-12-inch-by-2-inch-deep baking dish with olive oil spray.
2. In a medium bowl, toss the squash with 2 teaspoons oil, rose-

mary, and freshly ground black pepper. Place the well-coated squash slices on the tray and bake for 15–18 minutes or until cooked. Set aside.

3. In a medium, heavy-based saucepan, heat the remaining oil. Add the onion and carrot, and cook, stirring occasionally, for 5 minutes. Add the garlic, tomato paste, and tomatoes, bring to a boil, then reduce heat to low, and simmer gently for 5 minutes. Add the lentils and sugar and cook for 5 minutes or until the carrot is tender. Remove from the heat and stir in the spinach and parsley.

4. In a small bowl, combine the ricotta, egg, milk, and ¼ cup of the Parmesan cheese. Season with pepper and mix together well.

5. Spoon ⅔ cup of the lentil sauce over the base of the baking dish and spread evenly. Lay 3 lasagna noodles evenly over this. Spread 1 cup of lentil sauce over the lasagna noodles, then half the squash, and then ⅓ of the ricotta mix. Repeat layering with the lasagna noodles, 1 cup of the lentil sauce, the remaining squash, and then ⅓ of the ricotta mix. (You may need to break up some of the lasagna noodles to fit over the sauce). Lay the remaining lasagna noodles over the top. Top with the remaining lentil mix and then the ricotta mix. Sprinkle with the remaining Parmesan cheese.

6. Cover the dish with foil and bake for 30 minutes. Uncover and bake for another 30–35 minutes or until top is golden. Cut into 8 even portions and serve with lots of crispy green salad.

◄ PER SERVING FOR 8 SERVINGS WITHOUT SALAD ►
289 cal; 11 g fat (including 5.5 g saturated fat); 3 g fiber;
16 g protein; 30 g carbohydrates

VEGETARIAN PAD THAI

*T*he secret for successful Asian cooking is to have all the ingredients prepared and ready in front of you before you start cooking.

SERVES 4 ■ **PREPARATION TIME** 25 minutes ■ **MARINATING TIME** 30 minutes
■ **COOKING TIME** 15 minutes + standing time

---

10 ounces firm tofu, drained, cut into cubes
¼ cup gluten-free reduced-salt tamari
2 teaspoons gluten-free plum sauce
1 clove garlic, crushed
1 teaspoon finely grated fresh ginger
2½ tablespoons lime juice
1 teaspoon superfine sugar
7 ounces gluten-free dried rice-stick noodles
1½ tablespoons canola oil
1 onion, cut into thin wedges
1 long red chili, deseeded, cut into thin strips
1 red pepper, thinly sliced
3½ ounces bean sprouts, trimmed
¼ cup chopped garlic chives
¼ cup chopped cilantro
1 scallion, thinly sliced

To Serve
¼ cup chopped toasted cashews
lime wedges

1. Place the tofu in a shallow, nonmetallic dish. In a small bowl,
   combine 2 tablespoons of the tamari with the plum sauce, garlic, and ginger. Pour the tamari marinade over the tofu, cover,
   and set aside in the refrigerator to marinate for at least 30
   minutes.
2. Place the remaining tamari, lime juice, and sugar in a small
   bowl and stir with a fork to combine. Set aside.
3. Place the noodles in a large heatproof bowl and pour over
   enough boiling water to cover. Let stand for 5 minutes, then
   drain and set aside.

4. Heat half the oil in a wok over high heat. With a slotted spoon, add the tofu in batches and cook for 2–3 minutes or until golden brown. Remove from the wok and set aside in a clean bowl. Reserve any remaining tofu marinade.

5. Add the remaining oil to the wok with the onion and chili, and stir-fry for 2 minutes. Add the peppers and bean sprouts and stir-fry for 1 minute more.

6. Add the noodles and lime juice mixture to the wok and toss gently over high heat for 2 minutes or until noodles are coated in the sauce and heated through. Return the tofu to the wok with the reserved tofu marinade, garlic chives, cilantro, and scallion, and cook for 1 minute more.

7. Spoon the Pad Thai into bowls and serve topped with cashews and accompanied by lime wedges.

◄ PER SERVING ►
370 cal; 15 g fat (including 2 g saturated fat); 4 g fiber;
16 g protein; 40 g carbohydrates

▪12▪
Desserts

*S*weet endings like these desserts can help you increase
your intake of deliciously healthy, low-GI fruits and low-
fat dairy foods.

Of course, some of them are to keep for very special occasions!

BERRY AND PEAR COBBLER

*T*his is a traditional winter warmer. Serve with a dollop of low-fat ice cream or vanilla yogurt for an old-fashioned treat.

SERVES 4 ■ PREPARATION TIME 20 minutes ■
COOKING TIME 30–35 minutes + cooling time

---

10 ounces frozen mixed berries
14-ounce can pears in natural juice, drained and sliced
2 teaspoons superfine sugar

Topping
½ cup brown rice flour
⅓ cup gluten-free cornstarch
2 teaspoons gluten-free baking powder
½ teaspoon xanthan gum
¼ cup superfine sugar
2 teaspoons psyllium husks
2½ tablespoons reduced-fat margarine
¼ cup buttermilk
1 teaspoon vanilla extract
2½ tablespoons almond meal

To Serve
low-fat ice cream or vanilla yogurt

1. Preheat the oven to 350°F. Mix together the berries, pear slices, and sugar, and spoon into a 6-cup-capacity (2-in high) oven-proof dish.

2. To make the topping, sift the flour, cornstarch, baking powder, and xanthan gum into a medium bowl, stir to combine the mixture and then sift again into another bowl. Stir in the sugar and psyllium husks. Rub the margarine into the flour mix until it resembles breadcrumbs.

3. Combine the buttermilk and vanilla extract in a small bowl. Pour into the flour mixture and mix with a palette knife, using a cutting motion, until the mixture comes together. Knead quickly and lightly for a few seconds to make a smooth dough.

4. Divide the dough into 8 small portions. Form each portion into a ball and then flatten slightly to make a "scone" shape.

5. Sprinkle the almond meal evenly over the fruit mix. Place the dough shapes over the top. (It won't cover the fruit completely—this doesn't matter, because the fruit bubbles up around the scones.) Bake for 30–35 minutes or until the top is a light golden brown. Let stand for 5 minutes before serving with ice cream or yogurt.

◄ PER SERVING WITHOUT ICE CREAM ►
285 cal; 7 g fat (including 1 g saturated fat); 5 g fiber;
5 g protein; 50 g carbohydrates

BERRY YOGURT DELIGHT

This is the perfect dessert when berries are in season. Frozen berries are a good substitute when they're not in season, but you need to allow a little extra thawing time in Step 1. We originally intended to serve this dessert with meringues, but Diane tested it with amaretti cookies and it was so delicious and so effortless that we changed our minds! However, the meringue recipe follows, just in case you would like to try the alternative.

SERVES 4 ■ PREPARATION TIME 15 minutes

---

5 ounces (1 pint) strawberries
5½ ounces (1 pint) blueberries or raspberries
1½ tablespoons runny honey
10 ounces low-fat plain yogurt
2 tablespoons superfine sugar
1 teaspoon finely grated lime zest
8 (about 1 ounce) gluten-free amaretti cookies, crushed lightly

1. Wash, dry, and hull the strawberries. Slice them and combine in a bowl with the blueberries and honey. Whisk the yogurt with the sugar and lime zest. Taste for sweetness and add a little more sugar if needed.
2. Divide the berries evenly among 4 dessert dishes, spoon over 2–3 tablespoons of yogurt mixture, top with a sprinkling of crushed amaretti cookies, and serve immediately.

◄ PER SERVING ►
155 cal; 1 g fat (negligible saturated fat); 2.5 g fiber;
6 g protein; 29 g carbohydrates

MERINGUES

MAKES 24 ■ PREPARATION TIME 15 minutes ■
COOKING TIME 1 hour + 2 hours cooling time

---

2 egg whites
½ cup superfine sugar
½ teaspoon vanilla extract
¼ cup toasted almond flakes

1. Preheat the oven to 250°F. Line 2 baking trays with parchment paper.
2. In a large bowl, beat the egg whites until soft peaks form. Gradually add the sugar, beating after each addition. Beat for 1 extra minute. Fold in the vanilla extract and almonds.
3. Place tablespoons of the mixture 1–1½ inches apart on the trays. Bake for 1 hour. Leave in the oven to cool with the door ajar. Store the cooled meringues in an airtight container.

◄ PER MERINGUE ►
26 cal; 1 g fat (no saturated fat); 0 g fiber; 0.5 g protein; 4 g carbohydrates

CHOCOLATE MOUSSE

*T*his is the simplest and most decadent-tasting chocolate mousse recipe you'll ever make. It's foolproof, made in minutes, and just needs about 2 hours' chilling to set before serving. It has lots of saturated fat, so do keep it for a very special treat only.

SERVES 4 ■ PREPARATION TIME 5 minutes ■ COOKING TIME 5 minutes + cooling time ■ CHILLING TIME 2 hours

---

3½ ounces dark chocolate (63% cocoa), roughly chopped
⅓ cup reduced-fat evaporated milk
½ teaspoon vanilla extract
6 ounces reduced-fat, honey-flavored yogurt

1. Place the chocolate and milk in a heatproof bowl. Place over a saucepan of simmering water and stir until chocolate has melted and mixture is smooth.

2. Remove from heat and add vanilla extract. Set aside to cool for 5 minutes, then add yogurt and whisk until smooth.

3. Pour mixture into four or six ½-cup-capacity serving glasses and set in the refrigerator for 2 hours before serving.

◄ PER SERVING ►
4 servings: 186 cal; 8 g fat (including 7.5 g saturated fat);
1 g fiber; 5 g protein; 23 g carbohydrates
6 servings: 124 cal; 5 g fat (including 5 g saturated fat);
1 g fiber; 4 g protein; 16 g carbohydrates

PASSION FRUIT BANANA CUPS

SERVES 2 ■ PREPARATION TIME 5 minutes

6 ounces low-fat plain yogurt
1 large banana (just ripe), peeled and sliced
2 passion fruit
2 Coconut and Lime Macaroons (see page 207)

1. Spoon the yogurt evenly into 2 small cups. Divide the banana between the cups and top with the passion fruit. Serve with a Coconut and Lime Macaroon alongside.

PER SERVING WITHOUT MACAROON
120 cal; 0.5 g fat (with negligible saturated fat); 4 g fiber;
8 g protein; 19 g carbohydrates

VARIATION
■ To make *Mango Maple Cups,* replace the banana with 1 mango. To dice the mango, remove mango halves, one at a time, with a sharp knife by slicing as close to the pit as possible. In each half, score 3–4 lines vertically and 3–4 lines horizontally to form a hatched pattern. (Take care not to cut through the skin.) Holding both edges of the fruit firmly, turn each half inside out. The cubes can then be sliced off. Mix 1 tablespoon maple syrup into the yogurt.

◄ PER SERVING WITHOUT MACAROON ►
120 cal; 0.5 g fat (negligible saturated fat); 4 g fiber;
7 g protein; 19 g carbohydrates

CHOCOLATE ALMOND CAKE

*H*ave them guessing what the secret low-GI ingredient is—and we're not talking about the cloudy apple juice. Don't spill the beans before you enjoy the compliments. (This cake should be frozen after 1 day, as the lentil taste becomes stronger with time.)

MAKES 10 slices ■ **PREPARATION TIME** 25 minutes ■
COOKING TIME 50 minutes + cooling time

½ cup red lentils, picked over and rinsed
1½ cups unsweetened cloudy apple juice
¾ cup gluten-free self-rising flour
⅓ cup cocoa
⅔ cup almond meal
4 eggs, separated
⅔ cup superfine sugar
½ teaspoon almond extract
pure powdered sugar or gluten-free powdered sugar mixture (optional)

To Serve
low-fat vanilla ice cream

1. Preheat the oven to 350°F. Grease and line an 8-inch-base round cake pan.
2. Place the lentils and apple juice in a small saucepan. Bring to a boil, reduce the heat, and simmer, stirring occasionally, for 15 minutes or until lentils are soft. Set aside to cool.
3. Sift the flour and cocoa into a bowl, stir to combine, then sift a second time to aerate. Stir in the almond meal.
4. Beat the egg yolks and sugar in a large bowl until pale and creamy. Fold in the cooled lentil mix, sifted flour, and almond extract and stir to combine.
5. Place the egg whites in a bowl and beat until firm peaks form. Fold into the chocolate cake mix.

6. Pour the batter into the prepared cake pan. Bake for 30–35 minutes or until the top is firm and a skewer inserted into the center comes out clean. Remove from the oven and leave in the pan for 5 minutes before turning out onto a wire rack to cool. Dust the top with powdered sugar before serving with ice cream if you wish.

◄ **PER SLICE WITHOUT ICE CREAM** ►
231 cal; 7 g fat (including 1.5 g saturated fat); 2.5 g fiber;
7 g protein; 34 g carbohydrates

CRANBERRY BAKED APPLES

*S*tuffed baked apples are easy to prepare and a great way to boost your fruit intake. Try them with our other filling options at the end of the recipe.

SERVES 4 ■ PREPARATION TIME 15 minutes ■ COOKING TIME 40–45 minutes

---

⅓ cup finely chopped walnuts
⅓ cup dried cranberries
2½ tablespoons pure maple syrup
1 teaspoon cinnamon
4 medium Granny Smith apples
1 cup unsweetened cloudy apple juice

To Serve
low-fat vanilla ice cream or low-fat plain yogurt blended with cinnamon and runny honey or maple syrup, to taste

1. Preheat the oven to 350°F.
2. To make the walnut stuffing, combine the walnuts, cranberries, maple syrup, and cinnamon in a bowl.
3. Core the apples and run a knife lightly around the center of the apple (horizontally) to make a shallow cut. Stuff the apples with an equal amount of the walnut mixture and arrange them in an ovenproof dish that fits the four apples snugly. Any leftover filling can be placed in the dish. Pour the apple juice over the apples and cover the dish with a lid or foil.
4. Bake for 40–45 minutes, or until the apples are tender when tested with a skewer, basting apples with cooking juices halfway through. To serve, place an apple on each serving plate and drizzle with a little of the pan juices. Serve with ice cream or yogurt if desired.

VARIATIONS
■ For a stuffing recipe the kids will love, mix ⅓ cup chopped dried apricots with ¼ cup white chocolate chips and 1 tablespoon apple juice.

- Mix ⅔ cup raisins with 1 teaspoon cinnamon, 2 teaspoons brown sugar, ½ teaspoon vanilla extract, and 1 tablespoon apple juice.
- Mix ¼ cup chopped dried apricots, ¼ cup dried cranberries, ¼ cup chopped macadamia nuts, 2 teaspoons brown sugar, and 1 tablespoon apple juice.

◄ **PER SERVING WITHOUT ICE CREAM OR YOGURT TOPPING** ►
252 cal; 8 g fat (including 0.5 g saturated fat); 4.5 g fiber;
2 g protein; 43 g carbohydrates

LEMON DELICIOUS PUDDING

*L*emon Delicious Pudding really is delicious. The name says it all. For a special occasion when you want to end the meal with a tangy taste, this is the pudding to serve.

SERVES 6 ■ PREPARATION TIME 20 minutes ■ COOKING TIME 35 minutes

---

¼ cup rice flour
¼ teaspoon gluten-free baking powder
2 teaspoons rice bran
5 tablespoons reduced-fat margarine
½ cup superfine sugar
1½ tablespoons grated lemon rind
3 eggs, separated
2½ tablespoons lemon juice
1 cup reduced-fat milk

1. Preheat the oven to 350°F. Grease a 6-cup-capacity soufflé or ovenproof baking dish.
2. Sift the flour, baking powder, and bran into a bowl, stir, and then sift again to aerate.
3. Cream the margarine, sugar, and lemon rind in a mixing bowl until light and creamy. Add the egg yolks, one at a time, beating well after each addition. Fold in the sifted flour mixture and then stir in the lemon juice and milk, mixing until smooth.
4. Beat the egg whites in a medium bowl until firm peaks form. Fold lightly into the lemon mixture.
5. Pour the mixture into the prepared baking dish. Place the baking dish in a larger pan filled with boiling water to reach halfway up the side of the pudding dish. Bake for 35 minutes or until the top is golden.

◄ PER SERVING ►
193 cal; 8 g fat (including 2 g saturated fat); negligible fiber;
5.5 g protein; 25 g carbohydrates

COCONUT AND LIME MACAROONS

MAKES 30 ■ PREPARATION TIME 20 minutes ■ COOKING TIME 35 minutes ■ COOLING TIME 2 hours

1 cup shredded coconut
2 egg whites
½ cup sugar
¼ cup almond meal
1 teaspoon finely grated lime rind

1. Preheat oven to 325°F. Line 2 baking trays with parchment paper.

2. Place the coconut on a third baking tray and toast in the oven, stirring once, for 3–4 minutes or until golden. Set aside to cool. Reduce the oven temperature to 300°F.

3. In a medium bowl, beat the egg whites with an electric beater until soft peaks form. Gradually add the sugar, about a teaspoon at a time, and continue beating with each addition and then beat for another minute. Fold in the coconut, almond meal, and lime rind with a metal spoon until just combined.

4. Spoon tablespoons of the mixture 1–1½ inches apart on the lined trays. Bake in the oven for 20 minutes, swap trays around, and then cook for 10 more minutes. Leave trays in the oven, with the door ajar, to cool.

◄ PER MACAROON ►
35 cal; 2 g fat (including 1.5 g saturated fat); 0.5 g fiber;
0.5 g protein; 4 g carbohydrates

RHUBARB AND APPLE CRUMBLE

*E*veryone loves a crumble on a wintry night. It's the ultimate comfort dessert. We've added fiber to this one with rice bran cereal—it can be crushed lightly in a food processor. There's no need to process it to a powder, just chop up the sticks.

SERVES 4 ■ PREPARATION TIME 25 minutes ■ COOKING TIME 40 minutes + cooling time

---

2 Granny Smith apples, peeled, quartered, cored, and thinly sliced
¼ cup superfine sugar
¼ cup orange juice
1 bunch rhubarb, trimmed and cut into about 2-inch pieces
1 teaspoon grated orange rind

Crumble
1½ tablespoons rice flour
1½ tablespoons gluten-free cornstarch
⅓ cup almond meal
½ cup lightly crushed rice bran cereal
¼ cup brown sugar
½ teaspoon cinnamon
¼ teaspoon ground ginger
2 tablespoons reduced-fat margarine
¼ cup slivered almonds

To Serve
low-fat vanilla ice cream or yogurt

1. Preheat the oven to 400°F. Grease a 6-cup ovenproof dish.
2. Place the apples, sugar, and juice in a medium saucepan. Bring just to a boil, then reduce the heat to low, cover, and cook for 10 minutes. Add the rhubarb, cover, and cook for another 10 minutes. Remove from the heat, stir in the orange rind, and set aside to cool for 10 minutes. Spoon into the prepared dish (use a slotted spoon if there is too much liquid).
3. To make the crumble, combine the rice flour, cornstarch, almond meal, rice bran cereal, sugar, cinnamon, and ginger.

Rub in the margarine until combined. Stir in the slivered almonds. Spoon the crumble evenly over the fruit. Bake for 20 minutes or until the top is brown and crunchy. Serve with ice cream or yogurt if desired.

VARIATION

- If you are short on time you could use your favorite gluten-free muesli to make the topping.

◄ PER SERVING WITHOUT ICE CREAM OR YOGURT ►
356 cal; 14 g fat (including 1.5 g saturated fat); 6.5 g fiber;
6 g protein; 49 g carbohydrates

ORANGE ALMOND DESSERT CAKE

*T*his is a deliciously moist, dense, and rich dessert cake inspired by Claudia Roden's famous Middle Eastern orange and almond cake. It is very easy to make, but you do need to set aside the time to cook the oranges. It doesn't need an accompaniment, as it is very rich. This will keep for about 5 days in the refrigerator but is unsuitable for freezing.

MAKES 16 slices ■ **PREPARATION TIME** 25 minutes ■
COOKING TIME 2 hours 45 minutes + cooling time

---

2 large (about 9 ounces each) oranges, washed
14-ounce can chickpeas, drained and rinsed
5 eggs, separated
1¼ cups superfine sugar
4½ ounces ground almonds
1 teaspoon gluten-free baking powder
1 teaspoon vanilla extract

1. Place the oranges (skin and all) in a saucepan with a little water (enough to cover ⅓–½ of the oranges). Bring to a boil, cover, and cook, turning occasionally, for 1¼–1½ hours or until oranges are soft. Remove oranges from the liquid and leave to cool. When cool, quarter, remove the white stalk and seeds, and chop roughly.

2. Meanwhile, preheat the oven to 325°F. Grease and line the base of a 10-inch-base round cake pan.

3. Place chickpeas in a food processor and process until chopped. Add the oranges and process again until puréed.

4. Beat the egg yolks and sugar together in a very large bowl until thick, pale, and creamy. Fold in the orange purée, almonds, baking powder, and vanilla extract until combined.

5. Whisk the egg whites in a bowl until soft peaks form. Fold into the orange mixture.

6. Pour the cake batter into the cake pan. Bake for 1 hour and 15 minutes or until top is firm, cake is not wobbly, and a toothpick inserted into the center comes out almost clean. If the top of

the cake is turning too brown after the first 50 minutes, you may need to cover the cake with foil.

7. Remove the cake from the oven and allow to rest in the pan for 20 minutes. Turn out onto a wire rack, then turn the right way up to cool completely.

◄ **PER SLICE** ►
165 cal; 6 g fat (including 1 g saturated fat); 2 g fiber;
5 g protein; 23 g carbohydrates

Tips for Using Legumes in Your Baking

■ Canned legumes such as chickpeas are suitable for baking, but only for dense, robust cakes. Wash and drain beans well, then purée. Experiment with different types.

■ Use strong flavors such as vanilla extract, coconut extract, almond extract, cocoa, or lots of lemon, orange, or lime zest to mask the savory taste of the legumes. You might need to increase the amount of sugar in the cake by a small amount.

■ Chickpeas add a nutty flavor and a pleasant, coarse texture. They go well with lemons and oranges.

■ If flour is used in the recipe, use a commercial gluten-free flour, as these usually produce a better result with legumes than combining different types of gluten-free flours.

YOGURT STRAWBERRY JELL-O

*D*efinitely one for the children!

SERVES 4 ■ PREPARATION TIME 10 minutes + setting time

3-ounce package strawberry-flavored gelatin crystals
1 pint (5 ounces) chopped strawberries
1½ cups low-fat strawberry yogurt

To Serve
low-fat ice cream
chopped, toasted nuts

1. Combine the gelatin crystals and 1 cup boiling water in a bowl, and stir until dissolved. Place in the refrigerator to cool—but do not allow to set. (It is quicker to cool it in the freezer, but watch that it doesn't set.)

2. When cool, fold the strawberries and yogurt through the gelatin and mix well. Spoon evenly into tall serving glasses, cover, and refrigerate until set. Serve topped with a scoop of low-fat ice cream and a sprinkle of your favorite toasted nuts.

VARIATION
■ Replace the strawberry yogurt with low-fat vanilla yogurt.

◄ **PER SERVING WITH ICE CREAM AND NUTS** ►
216 cal; 4 g fat (including 1 g saturated fat); 1.5 g fiber;
8 g protein; 36 g carbohydrates

▪13▪
Basics

*S*tocks, **sauces, dips,** mashes, and spice blends to add that final flourish to a meal or snack.

HOW TO POACH CHICKEN AND END UP WITH A DELICIOUS CHICKEN STOCK, TOO

*C*hicken poached in an aromatic stock is ideal for salads, and the meat turns out so juicy and tender. Strain the stock and use it when making soups and stews.

PREPARATION TIME 10 minutes ■ COOKING TIME 15 minutes
+ cooling time

---

2 skinless chicken breast fillets
1 carrot, chopped into chunks
1 stalk celery, sliced
2–3 stems cilantro or parsley, roughly chopped
1 bay leaf
1 clove garlic, crushed (optional)
1-inch piece fresh ginger, chopped
1 tablespoon black peppercorns

1. Place the chicken breast fillets in a saucepan with the remaining ingredients. Cover with cold water. Bring to a boil, then reduce the heat to low and simmer for 10 minutes. Set aside to cool in the poaching liquid for an hour. When cool enough to handle, use a fork to shred the chicken or cut into bite-size pieces.

HUMMUS

MAKES about 1½ cups ■ **PREPARATION TIME** 5 minutes

1⅓ cups cooked or canned chickpeas
¼ cup tahini
2 cloves garlic, peeled
¼ cup lemon juice
2½ tablespoons olive oil
salt (optional)
freshly ground black pepper

1. Place the chickpeas, tahini, garlic, lemon juice, and oil in a small food processor. Process until well combined and smooth. Add 2–3 tablespoons hot water to thin the mixture slightly. Season to taste with salt and pepper. Store in an airtight container in the refrigerator for up to 2 weeks.

EASY GUACAMOLE

MAKES about 1 cup ■ **PREPARATION TIME** 2 minutes

1 avocado
1 tablespoon lemon juice
1 tablespoon snipped chives, parsley, or cilantro

1. In a small bowl, mash the avocado and lemon juice with a fork and mix in the chives, parsley, or cilantro.

POTATO AND CANNELLINI MASH

SERVES 4 ■ PREPARATION TIME 10 minutes ■ COOKING TIME 25 minutes

about 14 ounces small new potatoes
2 cloves garlic, peeled
14-ounce can cannellini beans, drained and rinsed
2 teaspoons reduced-fat margarine
¼ cup hot skim milk
2½ tablespoons chopped chives
freshly ground black pepper

1. Place the potatoes and garlic cloves in a medium saucepan and cover with cold water. Bring to a boil and cook for about 15 minutes or until potatoes are tender. Drain. When cool enough, peel the potatoes.
2. Mash the potatoes, garlic and beans with a potato masher.
3. Melt the margarine in a saucepan. Add the mashed mixture with milk and stir for 1–2 minutes until warm. Stir in the chives and season with pepper.

LENTIL MASH

SERVES 4 ■ PREPARATION TIME 5 minutes ■ COOKING TIME 25 minutes

1 cup red lentils, picked over and rinsed
2½ cups gluten-free reduced-salt chicken stock
1 tablespoon fresh thyme leaves
freshly ground black pepper

1. Place the lentils, stock, and thyme in a medium saucepan. Bring to a boil. Reduce heat and simmer for 20 minutes, stirring occasionally toward the end to prevent lentils from sticking to pan base, or until the lentils are soft and the liquid has evaporated. Season to taste.

SWEET POTATO MASH

SERVES 4 ■ PREPARATION TIME 10 minutes ■ COOKING TIME 15 minutes

> 14 ounces sweet potato, peeled and cubed
> 14-ounce can cannellini beans, drained and rinsed
> 2 teaspoons reduced-fat margarine
> freshly ground black pepper
> 1½ tablespoons chopped basil (optional)
> 2 teaspoons balsamic vinegar (optional)

1. Boil, steam, or microwave the sweet potato until tender. Place the sweet potato and beans in a food processor and process until roughly mashed. Transfer to a bowl.
2. To reheat the sweet potatoes, melt the margarine in a medium saucepan, then add the mash. Stir over low heat for about 2–3 minutes or until heated through. Season with pepper, add basil and vinegar, if using, and stir through the mash.

CHIPOTLE CHILI IN ADOBO SAUCE

MAKES 1 cup ■ PREPARATION TIME 5 minutes ■ COOKING TIME 1–1½ hours

> 7 medium dried chipotle chilies, stems removed
> ⅓ cup sliced onion
> 6 tablespoons cider vinegar
> 2 cloves garlic, chopped
> ¼ cup tomato sauce
> ¼ teaspoon salt
> 3 cups water

1. Combine all the ingredients in a medium saucepan. Cover and cook over low heat for 1–1½ hours or until the chilies are very soft and the liquid has been reduced to 1 cup. This recipe will keep for 2–3 weeks in an airtight container in the refrigerator.

Gluten-free Spice Blends

YOU MAY HAVE already discovered that many spice blends in your supermarket contain gluten in the form of wheat starch. That's why we recommend the Gourmet du Village brand for our recipes—apart from asafetida (which contains wheat starch) and blends that contain asafetida, Gourmet du Village blends and spices are gluten-free. See page 246 for contact details. If you'd like to make your own, here are recipes for popular spice blends used in this book, courtesy of Herbie's Spices.

ITALIAN HERB BLEND

4 teaspoons dried basil
3 teaspoons dried thyme
2 teaspoons dried marjoram
2 teaspoons dried oregano
1 teaspoon dried sage
1 teaspoon dried garlic flakes
1 teaspoon dried rosemary

MADRAS CURRY BLEND

5½ tablespoons ground coriander seed
1¼ tablespoons (5 teaspoons) ground cumin
3 teaspoons ground turmeric
2 teaspoons ground ginger
1 teaspoon ground yellow mustard seed
1 teaspoon ground fenugreek seed
1 teaspoon ground cinnamon
½ teaspoon ground cloves
½ teaspoon ground cardamom seed
½ teaspoon (or more to taste) ground chili
1½ teaspoons freshly ground black pepper

STRAWBERRY SAUCE

$\mathcal{T}$his is a much better version of the strawberry sauce that you get from the supermarket. And, of course, it tastes like real strawberries! It's so easy to make. Double the quantities when strawberries are in season (and more affordable). Pour over ice cream, mix through plain yogurt, serve with fruit, or use in place of chocolate sauce on a banana split.

MAKES 1 cup ■ **PREPARATION TIME** 5 minutes

1 pint (7 ounces) strawberries, washed, hulled, and chopped
2 teaspoons superfine sugar
Place strawberries and sugar in a food processor and process until smooth. Keep refrigerated.

The GI Gluten-free Tables

USING THE TABLES

*T*hese tables will help you put low-GI food choices into your shopping cart and onto your plate. Each entry lists an individual food and its GI value. We also list a moderate serving size, the amount of carbohydrates per serving, the GL, and whether the food's GI is low, medium, or high.

Although the tables list only gluten-free foods, on pages 227 and 228 we have included information about wheat-free but not gluten-free breads and breakfast cereals in easy-to-read boxes.

A low GI value is 55 or less.

A medium/moderate GI value is 56 to 69 inclusive.

A high GI value is 70 or more.

You can use the tables to:

- Find the GI of your favorite foods
- Compare carb-rich foods within a category (two types of bread or breakfast cereal, for example)
- Identify the best carbohydrate choices
- Improve your diet by finding a low-GI substitute for high-GI foods

 ◗ Put together a low-GI meal
 ◗ Find foods with a high GI but low GL

Each individual food appears alphabetically within a food category, such as "Bread" or "Fruit." This makes it easy to compare the kinds of foods you eat every day and helps you see which high-GI foods you could substitute with low-GI versions. The food categories used in the tables are:

 ◗ Beans, peas, and legumes—including baked beans, chickpeas, lentils, and split peas
 ◗ Beverages—including fruit and vegetable juices, soft drinks, flavored milk, and sport drinks
 ◗ Cookies and crackers—including commercial sweet cookies, savory crispbreads, and plain crackers
 ◗ Bread—including sliced white and whole-grain bread, fruit breads, and flatbreads
 ◗ Breakfast cereals—including processed cereals, muesli, oats, and porridge
 ◗ Cakes and muffins—including other baked goods
 ◗ Cereal grains—including couscous, bulgur, and barley
 ◗ Dairy products—including milk, yogurt, ice cream, and dairy desserts
 ◗ Fast food and convenience meals
 ◗ Fruit—including fresh, canned, and dried fruit
 ◗ Gluten-free products
 ◗ Meat, seafood, and protein
 ◗ Pasta and noodles
 ◗ Rice
 ◗ Snack foods—including chocolate, fruit bars, muesli bars, and nuts
 ◗ Soups
 ◗ Soy products—including soy milk and soy yogurt
 ◗ Spreads and sweeteners—including sugars, honey, and jam

▶ Vegetables—including green vegetables, salad vegetables, and root vegetables

In the tables you will sometimes see these symbols:

★ indicates that a food contains few or no carbohydrates. We have included these foods—including vegetables and protein-rich foods—because so many people ask us for their GI.

■ indicates that a food is high in saturated fat. Not all low-GI foods are a good choice; some are too high in saturated fat and sodium for everyday eating. Remember to consider the overall nutritional value of a food.

Ⓖ indicates that a food is part of the GI symbol program. Foods with the GI symbol have had their GI tested properly and are a healthy choice for their food category.

To make a fair comparison, all foods have been tested using an internationally standardized method. Gram for gram of carbohydrates, the higher the GI, the higher the blood glucose levels after consumption. If you can't find the GI value for a food you regularly eat in these tables, check out our Web site (www.glycemicindex.com). We maintain an international database of published GI values that have been tested by a reliable laboratory. Alternatively, please write to the manufacturer and encourage them to have the food tested by an accredited laboratory such as Sydney University's Glycemic Index Research Service (SUGiRS). In the meantime, choose a similar food from the tables as a substitute.

The GI values in this book are correct at the time of publication. However, the formulation of commercial foods can change and the GI can change, too. You can rely on foods showing the GI symbol. Although some manufacturers include the GI on the nutritional label, you would need to know that the testing was carried out independently by an accredited laboratory.

FOOD	Serving Size	Calories	Carbo-hydrate (g)	GI	LOW MED HIGH
BEANS AND LEGUMES					
Baked beans, canned in tomato sauce	5 oz	116	15	49	LOW
Black beans, boiled	2¼ oz	86	15	30	LOW
Black-eyed peas, soaked, boiled	4¼ oz	125	17	42	LOW
Borlotti beans, canned, drained	2¼ oz	92	17	41	LOW
Broad beans, boiled	6 oz	151	15	79	HIGH
Butter beans, canned, drained	6 oz	118	17	36	LOW
Butter beans, dried, boiled	5¼ oz	120	17	31	LOW
Butter beans, soaked overnight, boiled 50 minutes	5¼ oz	120	17	26	LOW
Cannellini beans, dried, boiled	4 oz	118	16	31	LOW
Chickpeas, canned in brine	4 oz	123	16	40	LOW
Chickpeas, dried, boiled	3 oz	115	14	28	LOW
Four-bean mix, canned, drained	3½ oz	97	14	37	LOW
Haricot beans, cooked, canned	2¼ oz	74	13	38	LOW
Haricot beans, dried, boiled	4 oz	126	15	33	LOW
Kidney beans, dark red, canned, drained	3½ oz	98	14	43	LOW
Kidney beans, red, dried, boiled	3 oz	119	13	28	LOW
Kidney beans, red, soaked overnight, boiled 60 minutes	3 oz	119	13	51	LOW
Lentils, green, canned	4¾ oz	87	13	48	LOW
Lentils, green, dried, boiled	4½ oz	96	12	30	LOW
Lentils, red, dried, boiled	4½ oz	96	12	26	LOW
Lentils, red, split, boiled 25 minutes	4½ oz	96	12	21	LOW
Lima beans, baby, frozen, reheated	4 oz	126	15	32	LOW
Mung beans, boiled	5 oz	152	16	39	LOW
Peas, dried, boiled	6¼ oz	118	13	22	LOW
Peas, green, frozen, boiled	5½ oz	113	13	48	LOW
President's Choice Blue Menu low-fat four-bean salad	3 oz	70	9	13	LOW
Romano beans	5 oz	44	9	46	LOW
Soy beans, canned, drained	15 oz	432	13	14	LOW
Soy beans, dried, boiled	18¼ oz	736	12	18	LOW
Split peas, yellow, boiled 20 minutes	6¼ oz	118	13	32	LOW
Split peas, yellow, dried, soaked overnight, boiled 55 minutes	6¼ oz	118	13	25	LOW

Ⓖ program participant

FOOD	Serving Size	Calories	Carbo-hydrate (g)	GI	LOW MED HIGH
BEVERAGES					
Apple and blackcurrant juice, no added sugar	8 fl oz	45	26	45	LOW
Apple and cherry juice, pure	4 fl oz	69	17	43	LOW
Apple and pineapple juice	4 fl oz	63	15	48	LOW
Apple and mango juice, pure	4 fl oz	63	15	47	LOW
Apple juice, filtered, pure	4 fl oz	65	15	44	LOW
Apple juice, Granny Smith, unsweetened	4 fl oz	50	13	44	LOW
Apple juice, no added sugar	4 fl oz	50	13	40	LOW
Apple juice with fiber	4 fl oz	60	14	37	LOW
Campbell's, 100% vegetable juice	6 fl oz	38	6	43	LOW
Campbell's, tomato juice	12 fl oz	75	11	33	LOW
Campbell's V8 Splash, tropical blend fruit drink	8 fl oz	110	27	47	LOW
Carrot juice, freshly made	8 fl oz	71	14	43	LOW
Coca-Cola	4 fl oz	57	15	53	LOW
Cocoa with water	8 fl oz	6	0		
Coffee, black	8 fl oz	3	0		
Coffee, white	8 fl oz	29	2		
Cola, artificially sweetened	8 fl oz	2	0		
Cordial, orange, reconstituted	1 fl oz	54	14	66	MED
Cordial with water, artificially sweetened	8 fl oz	4	1		
Cranberry juice cocktail	4 fl oz	67	17	52	LOW
Diet Coke	8 fl oz	1	0		
Diet dry ginger ale	8 fl oz	3	0		
Diet ginger beer	8 fl oz	1	0		
Diet lemonade	8 fl oz	2	0		
Diet orange fruit drink	12 fl oz	11	3		
Ensure, vanilla drink	3 fl oz	101	16	48	LOW
Fanta orange lite	8 fl oz	6	1		
Fanta orange soft drink	4 fl oz	64	15	68	MED
Fruit punch	8 fl oz	120	29	67	MED
Gatorade	8 fl oz	63	15	78	HIGH
Grapefruit juice, unsweetened	8 fl oz	84	18	48	LOW
Jevity, fiber-enriched drink	3 fl oz	101	16	48	LOW
Lemonade	4 fl oz	52	14	54	LOW
Lemonade, artificially sweetened	8 fl oz	4	0		

Ⓖ program participant

FOOD	Serving Size	Calories	Carbo-hydrate (g)	GI	LOW MED HIGH
Lemon squash soft drink	4 fl oz	64	16	58	MED
Mango smoothie	4 fl oz	61	15	32	LOW
Mineral water	8 fl oz	0	0		
Orange juice, unsweetened, fresh	8 fl oz	86	19	50	LOW
Orange juice, unsweetened, from concentrate	8 fl oz	86	19	53	LOW
Pepsi Max	8 fl oz	1	0		
Pineapple juice, unsweetened	4 fl oz	52	12	46	LOW
President's Choice Blue Menu Oh Mega orange juice	8 fl oz	130	30	48	LOW
President's Choice Blue Menu Orange Delight Cocktail with pulp	8 fl oz	70	16	44	LOW
President's Choice Blue Menu Soy Beverage, chocolate flavored	8 fl oz	160	28	40	LOW
President's Choice Blue Menu Soy Beverage, original flavored	8 fl oz	160	9	15	LOW
President's Choice Blue Menu Soy Beverage, vanilla flavored	8 fl oz	160	16	28	LOW
President's Choice Blue Menu tomato juice, low sodium	8 fl oz	45	7	23	LOW
Prune juice	4 fl oz	72	18	43	LOW
Rice milk, low-fat	8 fl oz	122	27	86	HIGH
Smoothie, banana ▦	8 fl oz	215	26	30	LOW
Smoothie, banana and strawberry, V8 Splash	8 fl oz	90	20	44	LOW
Smoothie, mango	8 fl oz	215	26	32	LOW
Soda water	8 fl oz	0	0		
Solo light	8 fl oz	5	1		
Sprite Zero lemonade	8 fl oz	2	0		
Tea, black	8 fl oz	3	0		
Tea, white	8 fl oz	16	1		
Tomato juice, no added sugar	12 fl oz	86	17	38	LOW
Tomato juice, unsweetened	4 fl oz	22	3		
Tonic water, artificially sweetened	8 fl oz	0	0		

BREAD					
Corn tortilla	1 oz	74	14	52	LOW

Ⓖ program participant

FOOD	Serving Size	Calories	Carbo-hydrate (g)	GI	LOW MED HIGH
WHEAT-FREE (NOT GLUTEN-FREE) BREADS					
Pumpernickel bread	1 oz	74	14	50	LOW
Schinkenbrot, dark rye bread	1¼ oz	102	18	86	HIGH
Sourdough rye bread	1¼ oz	96	18	48	LOW
Whole-grain rye bread	1 oz	83	15	58	MED
BREAKFAST CEREALS					
Puffed buckwheat	¾ oz	67	15	65	MED
Vita-Pro	1 oz	104	14	52	LOW
WHEAT-FREE (NOT GLUTEN-FREE) BREAKFAST CEREALS					
Gluten-free Muesli	1½ oz	183	13	39	LOW
Life, Quaker Oats	1 oz	120	24	66	MED
Oat bran, raw, unprocessed	1 oz	74	15	55	LOW
Oats, rolled, raw	1 oz	114	17	59	MED
Oatmeal, instant, made with water	6 oz	101	18	82	HIGH
Oatmeal, made from steel-cut oats with water	6 oz	101	18	52	LOW
Oatmeal, regular, made from oats with water	6 oz	101	18	58	MED
President's Choice Blue Menu Steel-Cut Oats	1¼ oz	150	29	57	MED
Quick Oats Porridge	¾ oz	74	15	80	HIGH
Quick Oats	6 oz	100	19	65	MED
CAKES AND MUFFINS					
Pancakes, buckwheat, gluten-free, packet mix	¾ oz	67	15	102	HIGH
CEREAL GRAINS					
Buckwheat, boiled	3 oz	89	17	54	LOW
Millet, boiled	2½ oz	83	16	71	HIGH
Polenta (cornmeal), boiled	6¾ oz	46	16	68	MED
Quinoa, raw	1 oz	84	15	53	LOW

Ⓖ program participant

FOOD	Serving Size	Calories	Carbo-hydrate (g)	GI	LOW MED HIGH
WHEAT-FREE (NOT GLUTEN-FREE) CEREAL GRAINS					
Barley, pearled, boiled	2 oz	74	14	25	LOW
Rye, whole kernels, raw	1 oz	67	14	34	LOW
COOKIES AND CRACKERS					
Cookie, chocolate-coated, LEDA ■	1½ oz	183	18	35	LOW
Corn Thins, puffed corn cakes, gluten-free	1 oz	89	16	87	HIGH
Puffed Rice Cakes, white	¾ oz	75	15	82	HIGH
Rice cracker, plain	½ oz	60	11	91	HIGH
WHEAT-FREE (NOT GLUTEN-FREE) COOKIES AND CRACKERS					
Kavli Norwegian crispbread	¾ oz	68	14	71	HIGH
Rye crispbread	1 oz	70	28	63	MED
Ryvita Currant crispbread	¾ oz	82	16	66	MED
Ryvita Original Rye crispbread	¾ oz	70	13	69	MED
© Ryvita Pumpkin Seeds and Oats crispbread	1 oz	98	14	48	LOW
Ryvita Sesame Rye crispbread	¾ oz	74	12	64	MED
© Ryvita Sunflower Seeds and Oats crispbread	1 oz	92	14	48	LOW
DAIRY PRODUCTS: CHEESES					
Brie ■	1 oz	102	0	★	
Camembert ■	1 oz	93	0	★	
Cheddar ■	1 oz	122	0	★	
Cheddar, 25% reduced-fat ■	1 oz	99	0	★	
Cheddar, 50% reduced-fat ■	1 oz	80	0	★	
Cheddar, low-fat	1 oz	61	0	★	
Cheddar, reduced-salt ■	1 oz	123	0	★	
Cheese spread, cheddar ■	1 oz	87	1	★	
Cheese spread, cheddar, reduced-fat ■	1 oz	72	2	★	
Cottage cheese	1 oz	37	1	★	

© program participant

FOOD	Serving Size	Calories	Carbo-hydrate (g)	GI	LOW MED HIGH
Cottage cheese, low-fat	1 oz	27	1	★	
Cream cheese ■	1 oz	102	1	★	
Cream cheese dip ■	1 oz	76	3	★	
Cream cheese, reduced-fat ■	1 oz	58	1	★	
Feta ■	1 oz	84	0	★	
Feta, low-salt ■	1 oz	113	0	★	
Feta, reduced-fat ■	1 oz	70	0	★	
Mozzarella ■	1 oz	91	0	★	
Mozzarella, reduced-fat ■	1 oz	86	0	★	
Parmesan ■	1 oz	133	0	★	
Ricotta ■	1 oz	44	0	★	
Ricotta, reduced-fat	1 oz	38	0	★	
Soy cheese	1 oz	95	0	★	

DAIRY PRODUCTS: ICE CREAM, CUSTARDS, AND DESSERTS

FOOD	Serving Size	Calories	Carbo-hydrate (g)	GI	LOW MED HIGH
Custard, low-fat	4 fl oz	102	18	38	LOW
President's Choice Blue Menu frozen yogurt, Mochaccino	4 fl oz	120	21	51	LOW
President's Choice Blue Menu frozen yogurt, strawberry banana	4 fl oz	110	20	55	LOW
President's Choice Blue Menu frozen yogurt, vanilla	4 fl oz	110	21	46	LOW
Tapioca pudding, boiled, with milk ■	4 oz	125	18	81	HIGH

DAIRY PRODUCTS: MILK AND ALTERNATIVES

FOOD	Serving Size	Calories	Carbo-hydrate (g)	GI	LOW MED HIGH
Condensed milk, sweetened, full-fat ■	1 oz	82	14	61	MED
Milk (3.6% fat) ■	8 fl oz	168	12	27	LOW
Milk, reduced-fat	8 fl oz	122	11	30	LOW
Skim, low fat (0.1%) milk	8 fl oz	89	12	32	LOW
Strawberry-flavored milk ■	5¼ fl oz	116	15	37	LOW
Vitasoy, rice milk, calcium-enriched	5 fl oz	77	15	79	HIGH

Ⓖ program participant

FOOD	Serving Size	Calories	Carbo-hydrate (g)	GI	LOW MED HIGH
DAIRY PRODUCTS: YOGURT					
Diet, low-fat, no added sugar, vanilla	11 oz	156	17	20	LOW
© Nestlé All-Natural 99% Fat-Free Plain Natural	6 oz	136	17	14	LOW
Yogurt, low-fat, plain	6 oz	111	15	35	LOW
FRUIT					
Apple	4 oz	58	13	38	LOW
Apple, dried	1 oz	69	16	29	LOW
Apricots	4½ oz	42	9	38	LOW
Apricots, canned, in light syrup	4½ oz	72	16	64	MED
Apricots, dried	1 oz	75	16	30	LOW
Avocado	2¾ oz	171	0	★	
Banana	3 oz	73	16	52	LOW
Breadfruit	2 oz	57	15	68	MED
Blueberries, wild	3½ oz	45	9	53	LOW
Cantaloupe	12 oz	80	16	65	MED
Cherries, dark	4½ oz	73	15	63	MED
Cherries, dried, tart	1½ oz	153	30	58	MED
Cherries, frozen, tart	3½ oz	50	6	54	LOW
Cherries, raw, sour	5 oz	78	22	22	LOW
Cranberries, dried, sweetened	¾ oz	62	17	64	MED
Custard apple	3 oz	64	13	54	LOW
Dates, Arabic, vacuum-packed	2 oz	78	18	39	LOW
Dates, pitted	1 oz	72	17	45	LOW
Fruit and nut mix	1¼ oz	158	17	15	LOW
Fruit cocktail, canned	5 oz	68	16	55	LOW
Grapefruit	11 oz	86	15	25	LOW
Grapes	3½ oz	63	15	53	LOW
Kiwifruit	6¾ oz	108	19	53	LOW
Kumquats	¾ oz	13	2	★	
Loganberries	2½ oz	51	4	★	
Lychees, canned, in syrup, drained	3 oz	65	15	79	HIGH
Mango	3½ oz	60	13	51	LOW

© program participant

FOOD	Serving Size	Calories	Carbo-hydrate (g)	GI	LOW MED HIGH
Mixed fruit, dried	1 oz	78	18	60	MED
Mixed nuts and raisins	1 oz	158	17	21	LOW
Mulberries	2½ oz	23	3	★	
Nectarine, fresh	4 oz	50	10	43	LOW
Orange	7 oz	78	15	42	LOW
Papaya	7 oz	66	14	59	MED
Peach	7 oz	69	13	42	LOW
Peaches, canned, in heavy syrup	5 oz	66	14	58	MED
Peaches, canned, in light syrup	4½ oz	73	17	57	MED
Peaches, canned, in natural juice	5½ oz	69	15	45	LOW
Peaches, dried	1 oz	80	16	35	LOW
Pear	4 oz	68	16	38	LOW
Pear, canned, in natural juice	5 oz	65	15	44	LOW
Pear, dried	1 oz	68	16	43	LOW
Pear halves, canned, in reduced-sugar syrup, lite	3½ oz	62	15	25	LOW
Pineapple	6 oz	69	13	59	MED
Plum	9 oz	103	19	39	LOW
Prunes, pitted, Sunsweet	1 oz	65	14	29	LOW
Raisins	¾ oz	60	14	64	MED
Raspberries	2 oz	29	3	★	
Rhubarb, stewed, unsweetened	3½ oz	19	1	★	
Strawberries	17 oz	115	13	40	LOW
Tropical fruit and nut mix	1 oz	120	17	49	LOW
Watermelon	10 oz	69	14	76	HIGH

MEALS, PREPARED AND CONVENIENCE

FOOD	Serving Size	Calories	Carbo-hydrate (g)	GI	LOW MED HIGH
President's Choice Blue Menu Chicken Curry with Vegetables ■	10 oz	190	11	26	LOW
President's Choice Blue Menu Lentil and Bean Vegetarian Patty	4 oz	170	27	55	LOW
President's Choice Blue Menu Rice & Lentils Espana Sidedish	2 oz	180	38	49	LOW
President's Choice Blue Menu Sesame Ginger Chicken with Vegetables (entrée)	10 oz	190	17	44	LOW

Ⓖ program participant

FOOD	Serving Size	Calories	Carbo-hydrate (g)	GI	LOW MED HIGH
President's Choice Blue Menu Vegetarian Chili	8 oz	200	34	**39**	**LOW**
President's Choice Blue Menu Yellow Curry Chicken (entrée)	10 oz	200	14	**25**	**LOW**
Sirloin steak with mixed vegetables and mashed potatoes, homemade ▦	10½ oz	309	25	**66**	**MED**
Stirfried vegetables with chicken and boiled white rice, homemade	10½ oz	344	62	**73**	**HIGH**
Sushi, salmon	2¾ oz	102	19	**48**	**LOW**
Taco shells, cornmeal-based, baked	1 oz	120	16	**68**	**MED**

MEAT, SEAFOOD, EGGS, AND PROTEIN					
Bacon, fried ▦	1 oz	38	1	★	
Bacon, grilled ▦	1 oz	49	1	★	
Beef, corned silverside	¾ oz	23	0	★	
Beef, corned silverside, canned ▦	1¾ oz	96	0	★	
Beef, roast	1 oz	44	0	★	
Beef steak, fat trimmed ▦	6 oz	356	0	★	
Brains, cooked ▦	2 oz	89	0	★	
Chicken breast, baked without skin	3 oz	140	0	★	
Chicken breast, grilled without skin	3 oz	150	0	★	
Chicken chopped, cooked	3½ oz	204	0	★	
Chicken drumstick, grilled without skin	1½ oz	78	0	★	
Chicken thigh fillet, grilled, without skin	1¾ oz	113	0	★	
Chicken wing, grilled without skin	¾ oz	37	0	★	
Cod, fried	4 oz	192	3	★	
Crab, cooked	2 oz	68	1	★	
Dory, fried	4 oz	203	3	★	
Duck, roasted without skin ▦	2 oz	156	0	★	
Egg, whole, raw	2 fl oz	77	0	★	
Egg white, raw	1 fl oz	15	0	★	
Egg yolk, raw	½ fl oz	53	0	★	
Flounder, fried	4 oz	201	3	★	
Ham, canned leg	1½ oz	45	0	★	
Kingfish, fried	4 oz	261	4	★	

Ⓖ program participant

FOOD	Serving Size	Calories	Carbo-hydrate (g)	GI	LOW MED HIGH
Lamb, ground, cooked ■	3½ oz	218	0	★	
Lamb, grilled chop, fat trimmed ■	1¾ oz	108	0	★	
Lamb, roasted loin, fat trimmed ■	2 oz	141	0	★	
Ling, fried	4 oz	204	3	★	
Liver, cooked ■	2 oz	158	2	★	
Lobster, cooked	2 oz	53	0	★	
Mullet, fried	4 oz	281	4	★	
Mussels, cooked	2 oz	76	4	★	
Ocean perch, fried	4 oz	210	4	★	
Octopus, cooked	2 oz	69	1	★	
Pancetta ■	¾ oz	40	0	★	
Pork, grilled chops, fat trimmed	3 oz	171	0	★	
Prosciutto	1½ oz	51	0	★	
Quail	2¾ oz	151	0	★	
Salmon, pink, no added salt, drained	2 oz	90	0	★	
Salmon, red, no added salt, drained	2 oz	119	0	★	
Sardines, canned in oil, drained	2 oz	137	0	★	
Scallops, cooked	2 oz	56	0	★	
Seafood marinara, canned	2 oz	67	3	★	
Shark, fried	4 oz	231	3	★	
Shrimp, cooked	2 oz	55	0	★	
Snapper, fried	4 oz	251	4	★	
Sole, fried	4 oz	206	3	★	
Spam, lite ■	2 oz	96	2	★	
Spam, regular ■	1½ oz	133	1	★	
Speck ■	3½ oz	212	0	★	
Tofu, cooked	4½ oz	96	1	★	
Trevally, fried	4 oz	234	3	★	
Trout, cooked	4 oz	164	0	★	
Trout, fried	4 oz	200	4	★	
Tuna, cooked	4 oz	213	0	★	
Tuna in brine, drained	2 oz	76	0	★	
Tuna in oil	2 oz	177	0	★	
Turkey breast, deli-sliced	¾ oz	34	0	★	
Turkey breast, smoked, without skin	3 oz	132	0	★	
Turkey leg, roasted without skin	3 oz	146	0	★	

Ⓖ program participant

FOOD	Serving Size	Calories	Carbo-hydrate (g)	GI	LOW MED HIGH
Turkey, roasted breast without skin	2¾ oz	117	0	★	
Veal, roasted, fat trimmed	3 oz	122	0	★	

NUTS AND SEEDS

FOOD	Serving Size	Calories	Carbo-hydrate (g)	GI	LOW MED HIGH
Almonds, raw	½ oz	79	1	★	
Almonds, roasted	½ oz	84	1	★	
Brazil nuts	½ oz	90	0	★	
Cashew nuts, raw	½ oz	76	2	22	LOW
Cashew nuts, roasted and salted	½ oz	83	3	22	LOW
Coconut, fresh ■	½ oz	37	1	★	
Coconut cream ■	4 fl oz	263	5	★	
Coconut milk, canned ■	4 fl oz	261	5	★	
Coconut milk, fresh ■	4 fl oz	302	4	★	
Hazelnuts	½ oz	84	1	★	
Linseeds (flaxseeds)	½ oz	46	2	★	
Macadamia nuts, raw	½ oz	96	1	★	
Macadamia nuts, roasted	½ oz	96	1	★	
Mixed nuts, fruit, seeds	½ oz	62	4	★	
Mixed nuts, raw	½ oz	79	1	★	
Mixed nuts, roasted, unsalted	½ oz	81	1	★	
Nut and raisin mix	½ oz	68	5	★	
Nut and seed mix	½ oz	81	1	★	
Peanut butter	½ oz	104	2	★	
Peanut butter, no added sugar	½ oz	107	1	★	
Peanuts, raw	1 oz	155	3	23	LOW
Peanuts, roasted	½ oz	115	3	23	LOW
Pecan pieces	1¾ oz	349	3	★	
Pecans, natural	½ oz	93	1	★	
Pine nuts	½ oz	91	1	★	
Pistachio nuts, raw	½ oz	79	2	★	
Pistachio nuts, roasted	½ oz	77	2	★	
Poppy seeds	¼ oz	26	0	★	
Pumpkin seeds, raw	½ oz	75	2	★	
Sesame seeds	½ oz	79	0	★	

Ⓖ program participant

FOOD	Serving Size	Calories	Carbo-hydrate (g)	GI	LOW MED HIGH
Sunflower seeds, raw	½ oz	75	0	★	
Sunflower seeds, roasted	½ oz	77	0	★	
Walnuts	½ oz	90	0	★	

OILS AND DRESSINGS

FOOD	Serving Size	Calories	Carbo-hydrate (g)	GI	LOW MED HIGH
Canola oil	⅓ fl oz	89	0	★	
Copha ■	⅓ oz	83	0	★	
Cream, pure, >35% fat ■	1 fl oz	120	1	★	
Cream, sour, >35% fat ■	1 oz	120	1	★	
Cream, thickened, >35% fat ■	¾ fl oz	70	1	★	
Dripping, pork ■	⅓ fl oz	83	0	★	
Ghee ■	⅓ oz	97	0	★	
Lard ■	⅓ oz	83	0	★	
Margarine, cooking ■	⅓ oz	72	0	★	
Mayonnaise	½ fl oz	56	3	★	
Mayonnaise, creamy, 97% fat free	¾ fl oz	24	5	★	
Salad dressing, homemade oil and vinegar	1 fl oz	178	0	★	
Safflower oil	⅓ fl oz	89	0	★	
Sesame oil	⅓ fl oz	89	0	★	
Soybean oil	⅓ fl oz	89	0	★	
Suet ■	⅓ oz	76	1	★	
Sunflower oil	⅓ fl oz	89	0	★	
Tartar sauce	1 fl oz	71	2	★	
Vinegar	½ fl oz	2	0	★	

PASTA AND NOODLES

FOOD	Serving Size	Calories	Carbo-hydrate (g)	GI	LOW MED HIGH
Corn pasta, gluten-free, boiled	1¾ oz	59	13	78	HIGH
Mung bean (Lungkow bean thread) noodles, dried, boiled	1¾ oz	53	13	33	LOW
Noodles, dried rice, boiled	2½ oz	75	16	61	MED
Noodles, fresh rice, boiled	2½ oz	81	17	40	LOW
Rice and maize pasta, gluten-free	2½ oz	99	16	76	HIGH

Ⓖ program participant

FOOD	Serving Size	Calories	Carbo-hydrate (g)	GI	LOW MED HIGH
Rice vermicelli noodles, dried, boiled, Chinese	2 oz	75	16	58	MED
Soba noodles, instant, served in soup	1¾ oz	62	14	46	LOW
Spaghetti, gluten-free, canned in tomato sauce	4 oz	69	14	68	MED

RICE

FOOD	Serving Size	Calories	Carbo-hydrate (g)	GI	LOW MED HIGH
Basmati rice, white, boiled, Mahatma	2 oz	82	18	58	MED
Broken rice, Thai, white, cooked in rice cooker	2 oz	82	18	86	HIGH
Brown Pelde rice, boiled	2 oz	92	19	76	HIGH
Calrose rice, brown, medium-grain, boiled	2 oz	92	19	87	HIGH
Calrose rice, white, medium-grain, boiled	2 oz	92	19	83	HIGH
Glutinous rice, white, cooked in rice cooker	2 oz	82	18	98	HIGH
Instant rice, white, cooked 6 minutes with water	2 oz	82	18	87	HIGH
Jasmine rice, white, long-grain, cooked in rice cooker	2 oz	82	18	109	HIGH
Long-grain rice, white, Mahatma, boiled 15 minutes	2 oz	82	18	50	LOW
Uncle Ben's Converted, white	1¾ oz	170	34	45	LOW
Uncle Ben's Converted, white, long-grain, boiled 20–30 minutes	1¾ oz	170	34	50	LOW
Uncle Ben's Ready Whole-grain Brown Rice (pouch)	5 oz	220	39	48	LOW
Uncle Ben's Ready Rice Original Long-grain (pouch)	5 oz	230	43	48	LOW
Uncle Ben's Spanish Style, Ready Rice (pouch)	5 oz	240	43	51	LOW
Wild rice, boiled	2½ oz	70	13	57	MED

SNACK FOODS

FOOD	Serving Size	Calories	Carbo-hydrate (g)	GI	LOW MED HIGH
Apricot and Apple Fruit Strips	¾ oz	71	16	29	LOW
Cadbury's milk chocolate, plain ■	1 oz	147	16	49	LOW
Cashew nuts, salted	1¾ oz	319	13	22	LOW
Chocolate, dark, Dove ■	1 oz	170	23	23	LOW

Ⓖ program participant

FOOD	Serving Size	Calories	Carbo-hydrate (g)	GI	LOW MED HIGH
Chocolate, dark, plain, regular ▦	1 oz	144	16	41	LOW
Chocolate, milk, plain, Nestlé ▦	1 oz	145	17	42	LOW
Chocolate, milk, plain, reduced-sugar ▦	1 oz	108	17	35	LOW
Chocolate, milk, plain, regular ▦	1 oz	145	17	41	LOW
Chocolate, milk, plain, with fructose instead of regular sugar ▦	1 oz	145	17	20	LOW
Chocolate candy, sugar-free, Dove ▦	1 oz	149	14	23	LOW
Clif bar, Chocolate Brownie Energy bar ▦	2¼ oz	240	45	57	MED
Corn chips, Nachips	1 oz	150	17	74	HIGH
Corn chips, plain, salted ▦	1 oz	140	17	42	LOW
Jell-O, raspberry flavor	4 oz	80	18	53	LOW
M&M's, peanut ▦	1 oz	142	17	33	LOW
Marshmallows, plain, white	½ oz	48	15	62	MED
Milky Way Bar ▦	2 oz	260	40	62	MED
Muesli breakfast bar, gluten-free	¾ oz	97	13	50	LOW
Nuts, mixed, roasted and salted	7 oz	1230	16	24	LOW
Peach and Pear Fruit Strips	¾ oz	71	15	29	LOW
Peanuts, roasted, salted	5½ oz	871	14	14	LOW
Pecan nuts, raw	11 oz	2251	15	10	LOW
Plum and Apple Fruit Strips	1 oz	77	16	29	LOW
Popcorn, plain, cooked in microwave	1 oz	89	14	72	HIGH
Potato chips, plain, salted ▦	1¾ oz	271	27	51	LOW
President's Choice Blue Menu Flaxseed Tortilla Chips, Sea Salt	1¾ oz	250	20	45	LOW
President's Choice Blue Menu Flaxseed Tortilla Chips, Spicy	1¾ oz	250	20	34	LOW
President's Choice Blue Menu Microwave Popping Corn, butter flavor	1½ oz	160	31	72	HIGH
President's Choice Blue Menu Microwave Popping Corn, natural flavor	1½ oz	160	31	58	MED
Snickers Bar ▦	2 oz	280	34	43	LOW
© Sunripe School Straps Blackberry Sour Buzz	¾ oz	68	15	35	LOW
© Sunripe School Straps, dried fruit snack	¾ oz	72	17	40	LOW

© program participant

FOOD	Serving Size	Calories	Carbo-hydrate (g)	GI	LOW MED HIGH
SOUPS					
Black bean, canned	6½ oz	88	15	**64**	**MED**
Green pea, canned	9 oz	180	19	**66**	**MED**
Lentil, canned	9 oz	98	13	**44**	**LOW**
Minestrone, traditional	9 oz	140	13	**39**	**LOW**
Campbell's Country Ladle Minestrone, condensed, prepared with water	8 oz	180	28	**48**	**LOW**
President's Choice Blue Menu Soupreme, Carrot Soup	1 cup	100	13	**35**	**LOW**
President's Choice Blue Menu Soupreme, Tomato and Herb Soup	1 cup	80	14	**47**	**LOW**
President's Choice Blue Menu Soupreme, Winter Squash Soup	1 cup	90	15	**41**	**LOW**
President's Choice Blue Menu Spicy Black Bean	1½ oz	240	32	**57**	**MED**
President's Choice Blue Menu Vegetarian Chili, ready-to-serve	1 cup	200	29	**39**	**LOW**
President's Choice Blue Menu Vegetarian Chili Low-fat Instant Cup	2 oz	230	29	**36**	**LOW**
Split pea, canned	4½ oz	90	15	**60**	**MED**
Tomato, canned	9 oz	70	14	**45**	**LOW**
SOY PRODUCTS					
President's Choice Blue Menu Soy Beverage, chocolate flavored	8 fl oz	160	28	**40**	**LOW**
President's Choice Blue Menu Soy Beverage, original flavored	8 fl oz	90	9	**15**	**LOW**
President's Choice Blue Menu Soy Beverage, vanilla flavored	8 fl oz	120	16	**28**	**LOW**
Soy beans, canned, drained	15 oz	432	13	**14**	**LOW**
Soy beans, dried, boiled	18 oz	736	12	**18**	**LOW**

Ⓖ program participant

FOOD	Serving Size	Calories	Carbo-hydrate (g)	GI	LOW MED HIGH
SPREADS AND SWEETENERS					
Apricot spread, no added sugar	1 oz	56	13	29	LOW
Butter ▦	⅓ oz	0	0	★	
Cashew spread	⅓ oz	2	3	★	
Cottee's 100% Fruit Jam Apricot	1 oz	64	15	50	LOW
Cottee's 100% Fruit Jam Blackberry	1 oz	66	15	46	LOW
Cottee's 100% Fruit Jam Breakfast Marmalade	1 oz	68	17	55	LOW
Cottee's 100% Fruit Jam Raspberry	1 oz	66	15	46	LOW
Cottee's 100% Fruit Jam Strawberry	1 oz	65	15	46	LOW
Dairy blend, with canola oil ▦	⅓ oz	0	0	★	
Extra virgin olive oil spread	¼ oz	0	0	★	
Fructose, pure	½ oz	61	15	19	LOW
Ginger marmalade, original	¾ oz	56	14	50	LOW
Glucose tablets or powder	½ oz	59	15	100	HIGH
Glucose syrup	¾ oz	65	16	100	HIGH
Golden syrup	¾ oz	58	15	63	MED
Honey, Capilano, blended	¾ oz	70	18	64	MED
Honey, general	¾ oz	70	18	52	LOW
Honey, Red Gum	¾ oz	70	18	53	LOW
Honey, Yellow-box	¾ oz	0	18	35	LOW
Hummus (chickpea dip)	1 oz	73	6	22	LOW
Jam, sweetened with aspartame	⅓ oz	0	0	★	
Jam, sweetened with sucralose	⅓ oz	0	0	★	
Lemon butter, homemade ▦	⅓ oz	1	3	★	
Maple syrup, pure, Canadian	¾ oz	52	13	54	LOW
Margarine, canola	⅓ oz	0	0	★	
Marmalade, no added sugar	1 oz	61	14	27	LOW
Marmalade, orange	½ oz	37	13	48	LOW
Marmalade, sweetened with aspartame	⅓ oz	0	0	★	
Marmalade, sweetened with sucralose	⅓ oz	0	0	★	
© Premium Agave Nectar, Sweet Cactus Farms	¾ oz	64	16	19	LOW
President's Choice Blue Menu Twice the Fruit Apricot spread	½ oz	25	6	56	MED

© program participant

FOOD	Serving Size	Calories	Carbo-hydrate (g)	GI	LOW MED HIGH
President's Choice Blue Menu Twice the Fruit Strawberry & Rhubarb spread	½ oz	25	6	**69**	**MED**
Raspberry spread, no added sugar	1 oz	60	14	**26**	**LOW**
Strawberry jam, regular	¾ oz	53	13	**51**	**LOW**
Strawberry spread, no added sugar	1 oz	60	14	**29**	**LOW**
Sugar, brown	½ oz	65	17	**61**	**MED**
Sugar, white	½ oz	65	17	**68**	**MED**
Tahini	¾ oz	4	0	★	
Treacle	¾ oz	51	13	**68**	**MED**

VEGETABLES

FOOD	Serving Size	Calories	Carbo-hydrate (g)	GI	LOW MED HIGH
Alfalfa sprouts	½ oz	4	0	★	
Artichoke, globe	4 oz	28	2	★	
Artichoke hearts, whole, canned	1½ oz	14	1	★	
Artichokes in brine	1½ oz	12	2	★	
Artichoke hearts in brine, drained	3 oz	19	1	★	
Arugula	¾ oz	6	1	★	
Asparagus	3 oz	20	1	★	
Asparagus, canned, drained	3 oz	22	1	★	
Asparagus green/white spears, canned	2 oz	12	1	★	
Asparagus in springwater	2 oz	8	1	★	
Baby corn, cut, canned	1¾ oz	13	2	★	
Baby corn spears, whole, canned	1¾ oz	13	2	★	
Bamboo shoots, canned	1 oz	4	0	★	
Bean sprouts, cooked	2 oz	16	1	★	
Bean sprouts, raw	1 oz	6	0	★	
Beans, green	1¾ oz	14	1	★	
Beans, snake	2½ oz	21	1	★	
Beets, canned	6 oz	82	16	**64**	**MED**
Bok choy	3 oz	30	1	★	
Broccoflower	1½ oz	13	1	★	
Broccoli	3½ oz	34	1	★	
Brussels sprouts	2¾ oz	25	2	★	
Cabbage, Chinese	3 oz	29	1	★	
Cabbage, green, cooked	3 oz	20	2	★	

Ⓖ program participant

FOOD	Serving Size	Calories	Carbo-hydrate (g)	GI	LOW MED HIGH
Cabbage, green, raw	3 oz	23	2	★	
Cabbage, red, cooked	3 oz	26	3	★	
Cabbage, red, raw	3 oz	30	3	★	
Carrots, peeled, boiled	9 oz	84	14	41	LOW
Cauliflower	3 oz	21	2	★	
Celery, cooked	2½ oz	13	2	★	
Celery, raw	1 oz	5	1	★	
Champignons, whole, canned	2 oz	18	1	★	
Chili, banana, cooked	1¾ oz	10	1	★	
Chili, banana, raw	2 oz	10	1	★	
Chili, hot thin, cooked	¾ oz	6	1	★	
Chili, hot thin, raw	1 oz	9	1	★	
Chives	¼ oz	1	0	★	
Choko, raw	1½ oz	9	2	★	
Cucumber	1 oz	3	0	★	
Cucumber, Lebanese	1 oz	4	1	★	
Eggplant, cooked	1¾ oz	12	1	★	
Eggplant, raw	1½ oz	9	1	★	
Endive	3 oz	16	0	★	
Fennel, cooked	2½ oz	20	3	★	
Fennel, raw	1¾ oz	12	2	★	
Garlic	¼ oz	4	0	★	
Green beans, sliced, canned	3 oz	30	5	★	
Green plantain, peeled, boiled 10 minutes	4 oz	150	37	39	LOW
Green plantain, peeled, fried in vegetable oil	4 oz	194	37	40	LOW
Horseradish	¼ oz	4	1	★	
Kohlrabi	3 oz	36	4	★	
Kumara, boiled	3 oz	63	13	77	HIGH
Leeks, cooked	3 oz	27	3	★	
Leeks, raw	3 oz	28	3	★	
Lettuce, iceberg	¾ oz	2	0	★	
Lettuce, mignonette	¾ oz	4	0	★	
Lettuce, romaine	¾ oz	5	0	★	
Mixed vegetables, Chinese, canned	3 oz	26	5	★	
Mushrooms	1¼ oz	11	1	★	
Mushrooms, canned	1 oz	11	1	★	

Ⓖ program participant

FOOD	Serving Size	Calories	Carbo-hydrate (g)	GI	LOW MED HIGH
Mushrooms, shiitake, canned	1 oz	8	1	★	
Okra	3 oz	29	1	★	
Onion	1 oz	13	2	★	
Onions, canned, sautéed and diced	1¾ oz	26	3	★	
Onions, sautéed and diced	½ oz	6	1	★	
Parsley, cooked	1½ oz	10	0	★	
Parsley, raw	¼ oz	1	0	★	
Parsnips, boiled	2¾ oz	16	8	52	LOW
Peas, green	7 oz	128	15	45	LOW
Pepper, green, canned	1½ oz	8	1	★	
Pepper, green, raw	1½ oz	7	1	★	
Pepper, red, canned	1½ oz	12	2	★	
Pepper, red, cooked	1½ oz	11	2	★	
Potato, baked, without skin	3½ oz	72	14	85	HIGH
Potato chips, deep-fried	1½ oz	126	14	75	HIGH
Potatoes, baked, Russet Burbank potatoes, baked, without fat	5¾ oz	168	41	76	HIGH
Potatoes, boiled	5¾ oz	144	36	59	MED
Potatoes, Desiree, peeled, boiled 35 minutes	4 oz	82	16	101	HIGH
Potatoes, instant, mashed, Idahoan	4 oz	170	16	88	HIGH
Potato, mashed, made with milk	4 oz	82	15	85	HIGH
Potato, mashed, made with milk and margarine	4 oz	117	20	71	HIGH
Potatoes, new, canned, microwaved 3 minutes	5 oz	84	16	65	MED
Potatoes, new, unpeeled, boiled 20 minutes	5 oz	84	16	78	HIGH
Potatoes, Ontario, white, baked in skin	5¾ oz	161	41	60	MED
Potatoes, Pontiac, peeled, boiled 15 minutes, mashed	4 oz	74	14	91	HIGH
Potatoes, Pontiac, peeled, boiled whole 30–35 minutes	4 oz	82	16	72	HIGH
Potatoes, Pontiac, peeled, microwaved 7 minutes	4 oz	82	16	79	HIGH
Potatoes, red, boiled with skin on in salted water 12 minutes	5¾ oz	148	37	89	HIGH
Potatoes, red, cubed, boiled in salted water 12 minutes, stored overnight in refrigerator, consumed cold	5¾ oz	148	37	56	MED

Ⓖ program participant

FOOD	Serving Size	Calories	Carbo-hydrate (g)	GI	LOW MED HIGH
Potatoes, Sebago, peeled, boiled 35 minutes	4 oz	82	16	87	HIGH
Potatoes, wedge, with skin	1¼ oz	118	17	75	HIGH
Pumpkin, boiled	7½ oz	96	15	75	HIGH
Radishes, red	2 oz	9	1	★	
Seaweed	1½ oz	13	0	★	
Shallots, cooked	1 oz	9	1	★	
Shallots, raw	½ oz	4	1	★	
Snow peas, cooked	2¾ oz	39	4	★	
Snow peas, raw	1 oz	12	2	★	
Spinach, English, cooked	3 oz	28	1	★	
Spinach, English, raw	1 oz	6	0	★	
Squash	2½ oz	22	2	★	
Squash, butternut, boiled	2¾ oz	30	6	51	LOW
Sweet corn, honey and pearl variety, boiled	2¾ oz	84	15	37	LOW
Sweet corn, on the cob, boiled	2¾ oz	84	15	48	LOW
Sweet corn, whole kernel, canned, drained	3 oz	90	16	46	LOW
Sweet potato, baked	3 oz	79	16	46	LOW
Sweet potato, peeled, cubed, boiled in salted water 15 minutes	5 oz	115	31	59	MED
Swede (rutabaga)	5¾ oz	66	18	72	HIGH
Swiss chard	4 oz	24	2	★	
Taro, boiled	1½ oz	63	15	54	LOW
Tomatoes	1¾ oz	9	1	★	
Tomatoes, in tomato juice	3 oz	19	3	★	
Tomatoes, Italian diced	4½ oz	28	5	★	
Tomatoes, Italian whole peeled roma	4½ oz	30	5	★	
Tomatoes, whole peeled, no added salt	4½ oz	25	4	★	
Tomato, onion, pepper, celery	3 oz	19	3	★	
Tomato puree	2 oz	20	3	★	
Turnips	1¾ oz	14	2	★	
Water chestnuts, drained	¾ oz	11	2	★	
Yam, peeled, boiled	2½ oz	79	19	51	LOW
Zucchini, cooked	3 oz	17	2	★	
Zucchini, raw	2 oz	10	1	★	

Ⓖ program participant

Contacts

United States

www.csaceliacs.org
www.celiac.com/catalog/
www.glutenfreeliving.com (magazine)
www.gluten-freelinks.com

Canada

www.celiac.ca

Overseas Sites of Interest

www.coeliacsociety.com.au
www.coeliac.co.nz
www.coeliac.co.uk
www.coeliac.com.au

www.glutenfreeshop.com.au

www.orgran.com

Food manufacturer Orgran is based in Australia but distributes internationally, so foods should be available in other countries.

Gourmet du Village Spices

Gourmet du Village spices are gluten-free, except for asafetida and blends containing asafetida. They are available at good delicatessens, gourmet food stores, and health food stores, or you can buy them online at www.gourmetduvillage.com.

Acknowledgments

*D*espite the digital age, publishing a book isn't one of those things that magically happens. There's a big team in the background researching, checking, commenting, designing.

So first we would like to thank Fiona Hazard at Hachette Livre Australia, who originally signed us up to write the book; Vanessa Radnidge, our publisher there; and production editor Anna Waddington. Thank you for listening to our ideas and bringing the book to life.

For this US edition, we are, as ever, indebted to our tireless US publisher Matthew Lore of Da Capo Lifelong books and his eagle-eyed team: commissioning editor Courtney Napoles, project editor Meredith Smith, nutrition consultant Kathleen Hanuschak, copy editor Antoinette Smith, proofreader Gerry Murano, and designer Pauline Neuwirth.

Diane Temple has played an absolutely key role in helping us put this book together. We simply could not have done it without her. Diane has been wonderful to work with, developing and testing the recipes to meet our nutritional guidelines. Nothing was ever too much to ask—even using legumes in baking cakes! And we are also grateful to her intrepid taste test team: daughter Ava and husband Ben Gerstel.

Producing up-to-date GI tables is no easy task. Thank you to all those who helped, especially Sydney University Glycemic Index Research Manager Fiona Atkinson, GI Symbol Program CEO Alan Barclay, and Katherine Corbett and the GI Labs team in Toronto who made sure we had the latest values for foods available in the US and Canada.

Last, we thank our families for their encouragement and support—Lee Dixon (Kate's mum, who read and commented on the manuscript and made lots of great suggestions), John Miller, and Roger Sandall.

About the Authors

Kate Marsh is an advanced accredited practicing dietitian and diabetes educator, with a master's degree in nutrition and dietetics from the University of Sydney and a graduate certificate in diabetes education and management from the University of Technology, Sydney.

Kate works in private practice in Sydney and has a particular interest in diabetes, insulin resistance, polycystic ovary syndrome (PCOS), celiac disease, and vegetarian nutrition. She currently chairs the DAA National PCOS Interest Group and the DAA National Vegetarian Interest Group and is completing her Ph.D. at the University of Sydney, looking at the benefits of a low-GI diet in women with PCOS.

Kate writes regularly for a number of publications, including *Diabetic Living*, *Heart Healthy Living*, *The Australian Vegetarian Society Magazine*, and *Orgran's Everyday Health Magazine*, and is co-author of *The New Glucose Revolution Low GI Guide to Managing PCOS* and *The New Glucose Revolution Low GI Vegetarian Cookbook*. She is a recent recipient of the DAA Young

Achievers Award and was a New South Wales finalist in the 2006 Telstra Business Women's Awards.

Jennie Brand-Miller, Ph.D., is a professor of human nutrition at the University of Sydney, and former president of the Nutrition Society of Australia. Jennie is chair of the Nutrition Committee of the Australian Academy of Science, the immediate past president of the Nutrition Society of Australia, the director of Sydney University Glycemic Index Research Services (SUGiRS, a GI testing service for the food industry), and chair of the board of directors of the nonprofit company Glycemic Index Limited, which administers a food-symbol program for consumers in collaboration with Diabetes Australia and the Juvenile Diabetes Research Foundation.

Philippa Sandall is the editor of *GI News* (http:ginews. blogspot.com), the official online newsletter published by the University of Sydney's GI Group. As a keen cook, writer, and editor, she specializes in food, health, and nutrition and has played a leading role in developing and publishing the *New Glucose Revolution* series since 1995.

Index